Live
amazed

Embracing the Gifts of God
in
Longing, Loss, and Life

By Carla Lake

Presented to:

____

From:

____

Date:

____

To anyone who has ever felt overwhelmed, I understand. Our dreams fade, our relationships fizzle, and our well-made plans fail. We want to run and hide, to take cover, to wait for the storms to pass. But that, my friend, is exactly when we must lean closer into God's embrace and cling to His gifts of great and precious promises. Gifts that enable us to share His divine nature, rise above the fray, and live with peace, purpose, and power. So, instead of running away, let's do this together! Let's step forward and welcome what God has already given us.

Contents

A Word to the Reader

*so that . . . you may become partakers
of the divine nature . . . (2 Peter 1:4b ESV)*

IT HAS NOTHING TO do with me. I mean, I know my heart. I know my willful, stubborn pride. I know my inconsistent attempts to be good. Yet, it is well with my soul.

Despite the corruption that is in the world . . . in me, I've been miraculously rescued, and my soul is nestled securely in my Savior's loving arms. That truth knocks me right out of my senses. Leaves me speechless, dumbfounded, amazed.

If I were to keep that truth always before me . . . if I were to live amazed, my life would be a sweet, fragrant flower of praise to my Savior. Nourished by His goodness. Blooming despite the struggle. Attracting others to *taste and see that the LORD is good* (Psalm 34:8).

But I don't stay amazed. Not consistently anyway. Not in a way that shows up in my day-to-day.

Yet, despite my wandering affections, God, in His mercy, continually beckons me. Softly and tenderly calling me closer, inviting me to embrace the life He offers. *(1 John 5:12)*.

But this invitation is not just for me, it's for **you** as well: an offer to run to God, to cling to Him, and to rest in Him in all circumstances; to find in Him everything we need, including power in our weakness, peace in our pain, and purpose in our lives.

Live Amazed - Embracing the Gifts of God in Longing, Loss, and Life aims to help us stand in awe of the Almighty God who is all-powerful and eternal, yet close and personal to each one of us.

It includes:

- A Prayer to Live Amazed
- Thirty devotions inspired by my personal journey with God
- Scripture readings that highlight the character of God
- *What about you?* questions to ponder as you examine your own walk with God

- *Praise Focus* prompts to steer your heart towards the amazing attributes of God
- *Before You Leave* chapter to help you fine-tune what living looks like to you
- *A Personalized Promise for You from God's Heart to Yours*
- *Stay Amazed Verses for Meditation*, because living amazed is a lifestyle, not just a book
- *The Amazing Gospel Story*, because that is where it all starts
- An index categorized by topics, so you can choose a devotion according to your current need

As you read these pages, may the incredible truth of God's invitation sink deeply into your heart. May you always live amazed to the glory of God.

A Prayer to Live Amazed

O Holy God,

I stand in awe of You!

Your creation declares Your glory;

Your sacrifice reveals Your love;

Your power knows no end.

From everlasting to everlasting, You are God!

You know me, O God.

You know from whence I came;

You know my innermost thoughts,

You surround me with Your love.

I stand in awe of You, O God!

Amazed that You invite me into Your presence,

A sinner, weak, and vile.

I am nothing without You,

And with You, I have all that I need.

Help me to stay amazed, O God,

Amazed at who You are and what You have done;

Amazed at Your precious gifts to me.
I thank You for Jesus through whom I am justified,
For Your indwelling Spirit,
And for Your great and precious promises.
O LORD God, I stand in awe of you!
May I never cease to praise You for all that You are.
In Jesus name, I pray,
Amen.

PART 1

Embracing the Gift of Peace in Your Longings

The Lord gives strength to his people; the Lord blesses his people with **peace**. *(Psalm 29:11)*

*I am leaving you with a gift—***peace** *of mind and heart. And the* **peace** *I give is a gift the world cannot give. So don't be troubled or afraid. (John 14:27 NLT)*

When God is the One Who's Waiting

IT WAS MEANT TO encourage me, but something about what my friend had written in her message made me uncomfortable.

I read it again.

"Keep strong until you learn what God has in store from all that has happened."

I winced. There it was again. The uneasiness. The feeling of undue responsibility.

My eyes fell on these three small, yet heavy, words: "until you learn."

I thought about all that I had learned over the past couple of years. Years where one disappointment after the other ran headlong into the other. Yes, it had been a difficult time, but I had not wasted the pain (or so I thought). I had learned . . .

God is indeed sovereign.

He keeps His promise never to leave me or forsake me.

He is far better to me than I deserve.

These major lessons had etched their way into my being. Was there more for me to learn? What was I missing?

As I read her words again, I realized something. My friend was not chiding me to learn more lessons or unearth more pearls of wisdom through the murkiness of life. No, she wanted me to keep my eyes open, waiting to see what God had in store for me.

It was that simple word "until" that really unnerved me. It spoke of the passage of time. It symbolized that there would be waiting involved.

And I don't know if you know, but waiting is hard.

Oh, it's not so bad at the beginning or when you know exactly how long you'll be waiting.

But when the time is uncertain, and all you hear is the slow moving tick of nothing getting much better, waiting becomes painful.

"The slow moving tick of nothing really getting much better." Those were my daughter's words as she explained what it's like living in a post-disaster zone. But they apply to mostly all of waiting. Nothing changing. Nothing getting better. Just waiting.

Waiting to see how God takes the messiness and works it out for good. Waiting for your purpose to become clear. Waiting to live that dream you know is tucked somewhere inside of you. Waiting to get your act together. Waiting to live fully . . . once you find the secret to balancing it all. Waiting for that elusive future that you wish could be your present. Waiting to be happy.

Just waiting.

So, that was it then. That was what disturbed me about my friend's encouragement. I was not looking forward to anymore w-a-i-t-i-n-g.

How long before God shows me what He has in store? I have tried to be brave. I have fallen on my knees in surrender. I have promised to trust His timing. But how much longer? Why won't He show me now? What is He waiting on?

Then, one morning as I climbed out of bed to face another day of waiting, it struck me.

What if God is the One who's waiting on me?

Waiting for me to stop waiting.

To simply step up and take what He has told me is already mine.

Consider what He has told me:

God's divine power has given us everything we need for life and for godliness. This power was given to us through knowledge of the one who called us by his own glory and integrity. Through his glory and integrity he has given us his promises that are of the highest value. Through these promises you will share in the divine nature because you have escaped the corruption that sinful desires cause in the world.

(2 Peter 1:3-4 GW)

Did you get that?

Please read that again slowly and contemplatively.

He isn't **planning** to give to me. He **gave** to me, so that I may share in the divine nature.

And this:

I have come that they may have life and that they may have it more abundantly. (John 10:10)

There it is again.

God has placed LIFE squarely in front of me. On a silver platter if you will.

LIFE—"the pleasant and fragrant fruit of communion with and enjoyment of God."[1]

A LIFE where sin has no control, where fear does not rule, and where love and power overflow. A LIFE that breathes peace and exudes contentment, each breath dancing in glad surrender to a sovereign God. A good God who has made it possible for us to have this LIFE despite the messiness of life.

I struggle to find the words to describe the blessedness of this LIFE.

Yet, many mornings, I get up and choose my own cocktail of life. A life filled with doing, striving, planning, and waiting.

While the offer remains: LIFE. Abundantly overflowing LIFE. Fresh every morning, every moment.

Just waiting for me to reach out and grasp it.

So why don't I?

Why don't you?

I invite you to pause and consider.

In your waiting . . . yes, I know . . . I know you're waiting. You're like me; we're always waiting for something. So, in your waiting, have you settled for your own cocktail of life, the one that's not mixed quite right, that leaves you yearning for more? Or have you claimed the highest and best LIFE that God has in store for you?

It's right there, my friend. Everything that we need.

What about you?

God has given you everything you need for LIFE. What's stopping you from reaching out and laying hold of what is already yours?

Praise Focus: God is patient as He pursues us with His love.

Do You Know God Well Enough to Trust Him?

I HAD GROWN TIRED of the long faces. For several weeks, every Monday morning would find my children grudgingly showing up for school. I decided to do something about it.

I was going to take Monday back. Reclaim it. Rename it. Rekindle the joy of learning in my children.

So, as they trudged down the stairs, I greeted them with the news, "Today, we are going to do something different!"

They had gotten used to knowing exactly what to expect each day. Their daily assignment lists were usually written in their spiral notebooks and, following our morning time together, each would focus on his or her list. For the most part, it had been working like a charm. They thrived on it. But this morning I had not filled out their lists; we were going to do something different!

We were going to have a more free-spirited morning! We would work together on a project as a family, have some fun along the way, refine our goals, and dive into God's word. They simply had to follow my lead and do as I say.

I thought they would be happy, over-the-top, grateful to be free of another dreary Monday.

But they were noticeably uncomfortable.

"What are we going to do?" my daughter asked anxiously.

"Can you just tell us what all we have to do first?" my son chimed in.

"What comes next?"

"When will we finish?"

The questions kept coming. My two children were thrown off of their expected normal.

Without any clear vision for the day, they just weren't sure. This day could go very well, or it just might turn out badly.

I held my daughter's concerned little face in my hands, looked deep into her eyes and said, "You just have to trust me. I won't give you more than you can do. You'll see. It'll all work out fine."

And then it dawned on me.

Isn't that the way I respond to God? We respond to God?

We want everything laid out nicely for us.

No fuss from us as long as we like what is coming up next. But, when we aren't sure we like where He is leading, well . . . we get a little antsy. Nervous. Worried.

Then, we start to question Him.

"How long, God?"

"When, my Lord?"

"Are you sure, God?"

I mean, who could blame us? Who is happy walking in the dark?

As I peered into my daughter's eyes, her anxiety melted away as she chose to trust me, and I smiled at the way God uses my everyday circumstances to mold my heart and remind me of His great truths.

My daughter chose to trust me because she knows me. I wouldn't expect her to trust a stranger or someone she barely knows.

I think as she looked up at my face, she remembered. She remembered who I was and all that I had been to her. Her trust was based on knowing me. Even though she had questions, she knew enough to know that I would always guide, protect, and seek the very best for her. She was convinced of my love for her . . . even when I pushed her to do hard things. She. Knew. Me.

And so, it begs the question, "How well do I . . . do you . . . do we know God?"

When you have questions that perhaps cause you to doubt, fear, or worry, what comes to your mind when you remember God?

In *Knowledge of the Holy*, A.W. Tozer claims that "what comes into a man's mind when he thinks about God is the most important thing about a man."[2]

Do we really believe that God wants the best for us?

Is it even possible to know GOD, "a spirit, infinite, eternal and unchangeable, in his being, wisdom, power, holiness, justice, goodness and truth"[3], like my daughter knows me?

Here's the sweet, soul-satisfying answer: God desires a close, personal relationship with us and reveals Himself to us through His creation, His Word, and His Son.

They know the truth about God because he has made it obvious to them. For ever since the world was created, people have seen the earth and sky. Through everything God made, they can clearly see his invisible qualities—his eternal power and divine nature. So they have no excuse for not knowing God.
(Romans 1:19-20 NLT)

All Scripture is God-breathed. (2 Timothy 3:16a)

In the past God spoke to our ancestors through the prophets at many times and in various ways, but in these last days he has spoken to us by his Son. (Hebrews 1:1-2)

Now this is eternal life: that they may know You, the only true God, and Jesus Christ, whom You have sent. (John 17:3)

But if from there you seek the Lord your God, you will find him if you seek him with all your heart and with all your soul. (Deuteronomy 4:29)

Pause a moment and think about it. God, the Creator, so wonderfully complex, whose ways and thoughts are infinitely higher than ours, desires for us to know Him intimately and *confides in those who fear Him (Psalm 25:14).*

As we draw near to Him, He draws near to us and promises that we shall "come forth as from a couch of rest, refreshed and invigorated"[4] and filled with childlike trust.

But sometimes we settle for a cursory knowledge of God. Knowing Him like we know a distant relative, but never taking the time or the interest to become so intimately acquainted with Him that we can trust Him like my daughter trusts me.

Do we know God in such a way that innocent, childlike trust is displayed in our lives? Does our knowledge and trust fill us with peace—*God's peace, which goes far beyond anything we can imagine*

(*Philippians 4:7 ISV*) and assuages our questions, doubts, and fears? Does our knowledge of God allow us to trust that He will sustain us through the hard times?

As amazing as it is to imagine, God makes it possible for us to know Him. Now, it's up to us to trust Him.

What About You?

How well do you know God?
Have you accepted a limited man-sized view of God,
focusing on only one or two of His
innumerable attributes?
Or have you embraced the God-designed invitation
to "plunge . . . in the Godhead's deepest sea" and
become "lost in his immensity"[5]*?*
What steps are you willing to take to grow
in your knowledge of God?

Praise Focus: God is incomprehensible,
yet He allows us to know Him.

Breaking Free When Your Strength Becomes Your Enemy

IT SURE IS SWEET, isn't it?

This thing called strength. As a matter of fact, it may be the most sought after, most admired, most coveted trait in the twenty-first century woman.

We all want to be strong! And why not?

A strong woman gets the job done. She has a clear vision of what she wants and a detailed plan on how to get it. She pushes on, no matter the obstacles stacked against her. She may be scared, but she is brave. Life may knock her down, but she gets back up, brushes off, and becomes stronger still. She is fierce in her loyalty, protecting the ones she loves.

You've seen her. You know her. Perhaps she's you. She appears in control, self-sufficient, independent, and seldom needs help.

And therein lies the problem: Sometimes, our strength becomes our enemy.

I come from a long line of strong women, and I see the many benefits. But I also see the pitfalls: an unwillingness, almost inability, to ask for help or to accept an offer of help; the secret disdain for weakness . . . in ourselves and in others; the pride that links arms with strength and takes you for a walk— a long, slow walk to a place you shouldn't be.

And it's not just us. Mr. Hyde of Strength has infected our whole society.

I see it in our young people, whose youth and vitality convince them that they are invincible.

I see it in our men who desperately desire to display strength **all** the time—a burden they are not called to bear.

Maybe it's time to pause; time to take a good look at our strength and examine its role in our lives. Is it a virtue or a vice?

Does our strength shine the spotlight on us and our successes? Does it keep us from asking for or receiving help? Are others intimidated by it? Does it keep us from being vulnerable, showing our weaknesses, or embracing community?

Perhaps we need to dig deeper. Take the cloak off strength. Expose its Dr. Jekyll and Mr. Hyde. Detect when the enemy of our souls is using it as one of his clever ploys.

For you see, sometimes we become so enamored by our own strength, so intoxicated by its appeal that we miss accepting the help that we need the most or saying yes to an offer of help we can find nowhere else.

The help we can never provide for ourselves.

Is that you? Have you fallen for your strength's trickery? Has it hindered you from saying yes to your Savior and receiving God's offer of salvation? From being saved from your sins and put back in right relationship with God?

Maybe you haven't ever considered it.

But, there your strength stands . . . the elephant in the room. Quite possibly blocking you from reaching out to God and relying on His strength, continually pressing in and trying to convince you that you are enough.

Yes, my friend, when your strength impedes your personal relationship with your Heavenly Father, it has become your enemy.

And then . . .

It is time to break free.

Time to shake off your strength, embrace your weakness, and endue His strength. Accept that there is a God, and you are not Him. Allow your weakness to shine the spotlight on Christ's power.

Be free to be weak.

May we find the courage to do so in the following verses:

My flesh and my heart may fail, but God is the strength of my heart and my portion forever. (Psalm 73:26)

But he said to me, "My grace is sufficient for you, for my power is made perfect in weakness." Therefore,

I will boast all the more gladly about my weakness, so that Christ's power may rest on me. That is why, for Christ's sake, I delight in weaknesses, in insults, in hardships, in persecutions, in difficulties. For when I am weak, then I am strong. (2 Corinthians 12:9-10)

The LORD will give strength unto his people; the LORD will bless his people with peace.
(Psalm 29:11 KJV)

He gives strength to the weary and increases the power of the weak. (Isaiah 40:29)

The LORD is my strength and my shield; my heart trusts in him, and he helps me. My heart leaps for joy, and with my song I praise him. The LORD is the strength of his people, a fortress of salvation for his anointed one. (Psalm 28:7-8)

The Sovereign LORD is my strength; he makes my feet like the feet of a deer, he enables me to tread on the heights. (Habakkuk 3:19)

Blessed are those whose strength is in you, in whose heart are the highways to Zion. They go from strength to strength; each one appears before God in Zion. (Psalm 84:5&7 ESV)

What about you?

Are you secretly proud of how strong you are?
Do you rely on your strength to nurture
others or serve God . . .
and then find yourself burnt out and exhausted?
How are you relying on God for your strength?

Praise Focus: God is all-powerful;
we can rest in His strength.

My Love Affair with Effort and Why We Must Break Up

EFFORT IS A BIT of a strange guy. At first, he seems so . . . right. He says, "You don't have to be perfect," and you breathe a sigh of relief! Now you can just relax and be you. What could be better? But then he adds, "You just need to try. And try hard!"

That doesn't seem so bad. As a matter of fact, it feels pretty good. The more you try, the better you feel. You feel accomplished and fulfilled. So when you don't succeed, you think, "Well, at least I tried my best."

Yep, Effort seems like a really nice guy.

As you get closer though, you begin to see the trouble. "All relationships have problems," you say, "we'll work it out." But these are some pretty serious concerns. Problems that have the potential to steal your joy. Serious issues that have caused me to reconsider my commitment to Effort.

Let me show you what I mean.

I've been with Effort a long time and, over the years, I've noticed something—my love affair with him has the dangerous potential to twist all of my relationships into performance-based traps.

My relationship with me:

Oh, I can get really tough on myself. Am I trying hard enough? Am I lazing around too much? Do I deserve this break? Did I do enough? You know how it goes . . . us work-'til-we-drop women. That's Effort alright; he pushes me to the max, and then wouldn't even let me enjoy some downtime. You can't stop now he says, there's more to be done.

It took me a while to realize what he was doing: chiding me when I rested, manipulating me into believing that rest is something I should earn, and blinding me from my Father's good intention for rest.

My relationship with others:

It doesn't stop with me. Without even realizing it, I check to see if others are as in love with Effort as I am. So, if this is what it looks like when I strive, I look at some poor, unsuspecting soul and, if perhaps he's working differently, I start to doubt his commitment.

Effort and I sit up on a pedestal—that critical seat of judgement. Together we muse, "Perhaps he needs to try harder."

Even when I'm serving others, Effort pushes grace right out of the way, twisting my motivation and stealing all the glory.

Yep, this love affair with Effort has been going on for a long time, causing serious damage between my loved ones and me.

Even as grave as that is, it's not the greatest threat.

My relationship with God:

You see Effort crossed the line when he tried to take the place of God, my true First Love. What's even more tragic is that I almost let him. As a matter of fact, it is a daily battle to keep him in his place. Effort restrained is quite a nice chap to have around.

He encourages you to work hard, reach your goals, and put your heart and soul into whatever you put your hands or mind to. He helps you motivate others. Why, he even supports your intentionality in spending time with God, your intended First Love.

But he is sneaky and, while I'm praying to my Father, he is whispering to me—trying to limit my expectations of God. Effort tries to convince me that I don't need to wait on God, that I can handle matters in my own strength.

If you're not careful, he seduces you, creeping up and up in importance until he becomes the one you worship.

So, we're breaking up . . . Effort and me. We can be friends, but the love affair ends here. I'm loosening the chains he has on me.

He won't convince me that my love affair with him is evidence of a successful Christian life or that I must deliver at a consistently high level for God's acceptance and approval.

He won't make me believe that my endeavors are somehow better or worse than those of someone else.

I will not agree with him and allow myself to be enslaved by others' approval.

Effort will no longer be permitted to steal my joy. You see, I've been with him long enough to know that no matter how I try, I can't find what I'm looking for with him.

No, my friend, only God through Jesus Christ, can give me . . . give you . . . that joy that we seek.

It doesn't matter whether you are a seasoned Christian, a new believer, or searching for God, Effort has a way of getting at us all. Perhaps it has something to do with our pride, that deadly sin that infects us. The faulty belief that we can somehow earn God's approval through our own striving, as if what Christ did for us was not enough.

No, make no mistake, slow dancing with Effort is dangerous. He undermines and steals our peace— the very gift of God that Christ died to give us.

There remains, then, a Sabbath-rest for the people of God; for anyone who enters God's rest also rests from their works, just as God did from his. (Hebrews 4: 9-10)

It is for freedom, that Christ has set us free. Stand firm, then, and do not let yourselves be burdened again by a yoke of slavery. (Galatians 5:1)

Oh, the joy of being free! I'm so thankful for grace and for the truth I'm learning more and more: "We cannot be truly happy unless God's acceptance of us is totally based on Christ."[6]

My friend, *if you think you are standing firm, be careful that you don't fall (1 Corinthians 10:12).* Hold firm to the hope that Christ came to give us; freedom that comes from relying solely on His righteousness, and let's keep Effort in his rightful place.

What about you?

Have you been hoodwinked by Effort?
Convinced there's something you must do
to earn God's acceptance?
Are you distracted from the truth of grace
by Effort's ploys?
And do you hold others to unrealistic
and erroneous standards?
Or are you happily resting in God's grace alone?

Praise Focus: God is merciful; we can cease from our
tireless effort and enjoy the fruits of His mercy.

When You Need to Forget Who You Are

THERE IS SO MUCH I don't want to forget. For example, it has been several years since I lost my father, yet I still have this fresh, urgent need never to forget the little details, his intricate nuances. And on a daily basis, I never want to lose sight of the reasons I started homeschooling or the real goals I have for my children.

Yes, remembering big, heavy stuff like this is important to me and brings clarity to my life.

But sometimes I need to forget.

Simply forget who I am.

I realize this may sound particularly foreign, even detrimental, in a culture that promotes the countless benefits of a healthy self-awareness and robust self-esteem. Nonetheless, I am convinced that there are times when a needle eye focus on me is the last thing I need.

For example, here are some instances when forgetting who I am may be most helpful:

- Life throws me a punch, and I'm caught in another fight, back against the wall, fists up.
- I'm so self-absorbed that I'm blinded to the pressing needs of those around me.
- My plans all fall apart, and I feel like a failure.
- I feel completely unprepared or ill-equipped for the task before me.
- I lose my joy to the dross of old or repeated sin.
- I'm paralyzed by fear and fail to think clearly.
- I wake to thick, suffocating grief that doesn't seem to fade away.
- I fall under the oppressive millstone of comparison that tells me I'm not enough.

Still doesn't make sense? Let me explain, and maybe you'll agree that you need to forget too.

In all these times, I become painfully aware that I can't do it on my own. That next to these problems, I'm very small. It is precisely why I must shift my gaze from me and my limited ability and fix it squarely on God and His limitless power.

I must **forget who I am and remember who God is**:

- The victor when it feels like I'm losing the battle *(Psalm 76)*.
- *The Father of compassion and the God of all comfort who comforts me in all my troubles* so that I can comfort another *(2 Corinthians 1:3-4, author's paraphrase)*.
- The Master Planner whose plan for me is far better than anything I can imagine *(Jeremiah 29:11)*.
- The One who is able and willing to equip me for whatever He calls me to *(2 Peter 1:3)*.
- The faithful and just One, always offering to wipe away my sins and *restore the joy of . . . salvation (Psalm 51:12)*.

- Love and His perfect love drives out my fear (*1 John 4:18*) (*1 John 4:8*).
- My *refuge and strength, a very present help in trouble* and nothing can separate me from His love (*Psalm 46:1*) (*Romans 8:31-39*).

This is the God I need to remember, the One who calls me His child, *fearfully and wonderfully made* in His image (*Galatians 3:26*) (*Psalm 139:14*).

Yes, when I'm wind-tossed by the storms of life, I need to forget who I am and remember who God is. He has an answer for every problem I face.

But these are not the only times I need to forget. Perhaps even more importantly, on the roller coaster of life, I must choose to forget who I am not only in the valleys but during the mountaintop highs as well. It is during these times, that I'm in danger of succumbing to the wiles of pride. I might actually believe that my success is all because of me and my abilities.

So . . .

When the birds are singing, the flowers blooming and life is rosy and bright, I need to forget.

When my family is prospering, my kids succeeding, accolades high, criticisms low, and I have more than enough for my family and me, I need to forget who I am.

Forget who I am and remember who God is.

Remember that *every good and perfect gift is from above (James 1:17)* . . . from our Heavenly Father and that it is not about me. Remember to give all the glory to God *(Jeremiah 9:24)*.

So, my friend, I hope you understand why I need to forget who I am sometimes. Focusing on me in bad times or good can leave me frail and fearful or entitled and ungrateful. **Only when I stand in awe of God and behold Him in all His glory and majesty, holding Him in the highest esteem and humbly accepting who He says He is and who He says I am, does it help to remember who I am.**

Set your minds on things above, not on things on the earth. For you died, and your life is hidden with Christ in God. When Christ who is our life appears, then you also will appear with Him in glory. (Colossians 3:2-4)

I am who I am because of Him. All because of Him and all through Him.

When my gaze is fixed on God and not me, then and only then, my sadness turns to joy, my fear to courage, my worry to peace, and my selfishness to love. I am filled anew with hope as I remember that His Spirit dwells within me, His power is available to me, and He delights in me.

Yes, remembering who I am is so much sweeter when I take some time to forget.

What about you?

*Are you in one of those times? One of
those peaks or valleys?
Do you need to forget who you are
and remember who God is?
I pray that you'll use this as your personal invitation
to take some time to forget today.*

Praise Focus: God is sovereign. He reigns above all.

Are You the One Who Jesus Loves?

"MY DEAREST C.J., I am waiting for you still. Find a way back to me, my dearest friend. I love you always. Merridy."

She snuggled next to me as I read those words, and we both smiled.

This is the third book in the *Growly Series*, one she had been begging to read, and already we could feel the thrill of hope and the surge of excitement. *Morning*[7] is a stirring fantasy filled with adventure, a perilous quest for love lost and deep friendship, all in the most magical, imaginary setting. It is an enchanting bedtime read.

As I closed the book and led our evening prayers, she nestled even closer.

"It's nice to be loved," she whispered, her eyes gleaming in the dark.

"Yes, sweetheart, it is!"

And then she added, "And it's nice to love, as well."

I beamed. Oh, the joys of bedtime conversations.

As I lay there, treasuring these moments with my daughter, my mind wandered through the intricate maze of all that love is.

I thought about my youngest brother. I had watched as my father believed in his son, valuing him highly and helping him to believe in himself. I had witnessed my brother's devotion to my dad and his selfless acts of service as he cared for him. All for love. As he lay in the hospital those final weeks, my father spoke a blessing upon my brother, "This is my beloved son, with whom I am well pleased."

I had smiled then, and jokingly chided, "How come you haven't said that about me?" But I had been deeply moved by the exchange between father and son, for I had seen the empowering love of a father for his son, and the self-sacrificing love of a son for his father.

Yes, it is good to be loved and to love, as well.

As I traveled through the pages of John's gospel, I thought about him, the beloved disciple, the one whom Jesus loved. I wondered, "Was it arrogance that made John refer to himself as the disciple whom Jesus loved? Surely, he didn't imagine that Jesus loved him more than the others?"

But the more I dwelled on his words, the more I noticed something special about John. I became more aware of his point of view, more sensitive to his perception. I could almost feel the depth of his realization that Jesus loved him.

I sensed his comfort, his abandon, like the ease of one fully accepted. John knew love . . . the love of Jesus and he claimed this love for himself. A love so real, so profound, and so personal that it defined him.

. . . the disciple whom Jesus loved . . . (John 13:23)

Who wouldn't be attracted to a love like that? A love that calls you, accepts you, empowers you, and gives your life purpose and meaning. Fully accepted and totally assured, John felt loved enough: loved enough to always stay close.

It was John who leaned back on Jesus during the last supper. Leaning on Him, perhaps even resting his head on His shoulder, asking the tough question no one else dared: *Lord, who is it? (John 13:25)* Just imagining someone betraying his Lord was distressing, let alone asking the question.

Loved enough to ask the tough questions and accept the answers.

John followed Jesus everywhere, even to the unexplainable, uncomfortable, unimaginable places: the Mount of Transfiguration, where Jesus dazzled them with His glory, the Garden of Gethsemane, where Jesus wrestled in prayer, and the Place of the Skull, where darkness covered the earth. Right there at the foot of the cross, as Jesus gasped for air, struggling to breathe, it was to John that He entrusted the care of His mother.

Loved enough to follow Him everywhere and to be trusted to care for the ones He loves.

It was John who received the Revelation of Jesus, a window into what is to come. Words that speak hope and purpose into our struggles, even now.

Loved enough to share in His secret thoughts.

Have you ever been loved like that? Loved enough? Love so rich and full that it answers a purpose or satisfies a need? Deep, intimate, life-transforming love?

I think John felt it.

He knew the sacrifice that Jesus made was for him. The decisions Jesus made—giving up all that He had, becoming a man despised by many, enduring an agonizing, humiliating death on a cross while separated from His Father as He became sin for us, trading His righteousness for our unrighteousness, making a way back Home for us, the lost and wandering—John felt that it was all for him deep in his bones.

Loved enough to die for.

This is love: not that we loved God, but that he loved us and sent his son as an atoning sacrifice for our sins. (1 John 4:10)

John felt it profoundly and personally. He never forgot it.

But it wasn't just for John. It was for you and for me.

Have you ever felt that love?

I think sometimes, I forget.

When I'm lost in the craziness of now, I forget that it was for me that Jesus died. I forget the Love that always pursues me, waits for me, and refuses to let me go—God's love. A Love that invites me into a deep, intimate relationship with my Father where I'm fully accepted and totally assured. A love that moves me to love as I am loved.

But I don't want to forget. I want to remember. In the moments when I feel anything but loved and anything but loving, I pray to remember. I remember that I am the beloved of Jesus. I remember that His love, wholly independent of my actions, has the power to transform me, to make me more like Him, and to empower me to love Him and others sacrificially.

I'm not there yet, but the more I yield to His love, the more I am filled with hope and delight and love.

So, just like C.J. in my daughter's new favorite series, we have someone waiting for us, loving us with a hope that never ceases, a love that's enough. But unlike C.J., we don't have to find a way back home ourselves. God has already given us the Way. We need only yield to His love.

What about you?

Do you truly know that you are the
one who Jesus loves?
Are you fully accepted and totally assured?
Do you love as you are loved?
Or, like me, do you sometimes forget?
What do you do daily to remember His love?

Praise Focus: God is love; He laid down
His life for us while we were still sinners.

Are You Really Fine Just the Way You Are?

"BUT SOMETIMES, YOU CAN rest and know that you are fine just the way you are; you don't always have to try to be better," my daughter said.

I came to a standstill and pondered her words carefully. I had this eerie feeling that I had stumbled upon a treasure—a nugget of great truth. I needed to linger here for a moment. I genuinely wanted to understand her and to take the time needed to sift through the dusty layers to unearth this pearl of wisdom.

I had simply said to her that there is always room for improvement.

We had been in the middle of a math lesson, and she had been dawdling a bit more than I liked. I had started in, yet again, reminding her that she could do better. It was a familiar tirade. One that I had repeated more times than I care to remember. Not only to her, but also to myself. We can always do better.

But my performance-focused reprimand was interrupted, shattered by the unexpected, much needed, soul-refreshing wisdom of a child.

"You can **rest** and **know** that you are fine just the way you are."

She had not intended it to be spiritual. But it was.

My daughter's words meandered through my mind and traveled down to the soft, squishy, most vulnerable part of me. The stirrings of my heart were almost tangible as I muttered the words, "Thank you, sweetheart. Thank you for your wisdom and for reminding me of a great truth."

I smiled at her bewildered face, turned, jogged up the stairs and without delay ordered the next book on my wish-list: *Breaking Up With Perfect*,[8] by Amy Carroll.

You see, there was a message in here for me, buried deep underneath the layers of an innocent remark. I was determined to dig it out, let it soak into my mind and spirit, and work its liberating magic.

And there were many layers. I would spend the next several days digging—exploring all the nuances of this loaded statement.

"You are fine just the way you are."

I knew I was right. You should always strive to do your best. Even so, deep down I knew she was right. My eleven-year-old daughter had unintentionally reminded me of the elusive harmony so many of us Christians search for. The need to cease from our labors and enter into the rest only Christ can give, while striving to *work out our salvation with fear and trembling (Philippians 2:12).*

After taking a few days to wander through the various roads this simple comment had led me, I returned to the conversation with my daughter. I wanted to gently scrape away the layers to understand what she meant when she said those words since she thinks deeply and is quite apt at expressing her feelings. We talked about how my love for her is not dependent on what she does but on who she is. She assured me that she was confident about this. (What a relief!)

Then we switched to the spiritual side of things and talked about law and grace and about how we are made complete in Christ, not saved *by* our good works but *for* good works.

And then, to prod just a bit more, I asked, "You're fine just the way you are, but shouldn't you always try to do better?"

Her quick reply: "Shouldn't you always think you're good enough?"

We were talking about two different things. Doing and being. The slippery balance that plagues so many Christians.

She went on, "No one is perfect. No one expects you to be perfect. If perfection is unattainable, then why do people still try to attain it? Yes, you should do better, but up to a limit, because 'doing better' becomes a burden. Like you have to do it, rather than you want to do it."

Now, I got it—the gem of truth God had hidden in there for me.

So many of us know the truth: *For it is by grace you have been saved, through faith—and this is not from yourselves, it is the gift of God—not by works, so that no one can boast. (Ephesians 2:8-9)*

Yet, we refuse to enter that rest. We don't articulate it, but the evidence is in our actions. We labor, day in and day out, always striving to do more, be more, until 'doing better' becomes a burden and robs us of the peace and rest promised to us through Christ—the only one who completed the work that we could never complete. When Christ *offered for all time one sacrifice for sins,* he sat down at the right hand of God *(Hebrews 10:12).*

He is now offering us that rest.

There remains, then, a Sabbath-rest for the people of God; for anyone who enters God's rest also rests from their works, just as God did from his. (Hebrews 4:9-10)

So why are we still striving so hard? Rejecting His rest? Beating ourselves up for not doing enough or being enough? Are we refusing to believe that what Christ did for us on the cross was indeed enough?

It's time to stop, my friend, and let the truth soak in and transform your life.

*Depend on God and keep at it because in the Lord
God you have a sure thing. (Isaiah 26:4 MSG)*

In other words, do the best you can, then leave
the rest to God.

It all comes down to trust. What are you trusting
that allows you to believe you are fine just the way
you are? Are you trusting in Jesus's cleansing blood?
Or are you trusting in your endless labour and self-
effort? Or a little bit of both?

*God made him who had no sin to be sin for us, so
that in him we might become the righteousness of God.
(2 Corinthians 5:21)*

Yes, when you receive God's forgiveness offered
to us through Christ, then those words that every
person yearns to hear can be true for you.

You really are fine just the way you are because
now you are **in** Christ.

You can cease from your labors and enter, with
all who believe, into the sweet rest Christ has offered us. You can be confident that he loves you not
for what you do but for who you are.

So, rest well today, my friend, and be reminded that the power of the cross makes you not just fine, but flawless.

What about you?

Has doing better become a burden for you?
Are you constantly trying to be good enough
to be accepted by God?
Or do you rest in Christ's perfection?

Praise Focus: God is merciful,
we can rest in His love.

Why I'm Thankful for the Labels That Challenge My Worth

B RISTLED.

No, that's not quite it.

Chafed.

Hmm - not that either.

Ruffled. Maybe that's more like it.

I love words. They are powerful. But sometimes they can be tricky.

I wish I could find the right words to match the muddled, confused soup of my feelings as I stared at the label on the application.

There it was, typed neatly under the box—Occupation: housewife.

For me, as a visual person, words in writing carry an extra punch. Compared to their audible counterparts, they embed themselves a little deeper in my mind.

Housewife.

The soup stirred. Prideful flesh was aroused.

I glanced at my husband. I wondered if he could sense my discomfort.

I bit my tongue as I wrestled with the impulse to qualify this label. Should I explain what else I was doing and justify why it was enough?

I was determined to win this latest battle in the long, drawn-out war on my worth.

I remained calm, said nothing and, pushing my pride back down, I left the bank. In the days following, the hard truth sank in—I have a long way to go.

You see, there are other labels. Labels that make my pride jump right up and pay attention. Often, with those labels, I don't squash my pride down, smug as he is. I allow him to stand tall and strut his stuff.

Even now, I am resisting the urge to tell you what those other finer sounding labels are.

Like I said, I have a long way to go.

My sense of worth cannot be grounded in pride's reaction. One minute it's up, and I'm smiling, the next it's down, and I'm frowning. It's like I'm on a see-saw and getting giddy from the ride.

Yet, I'm thankful for the ride, especially for the lows. I'm thankful that labels which challenge my sense of worth also cause me to stop, examine my heart, and face the truth.

Would you join me as I dig a little deeper? Perhaps we can do this together.

Stop and examine my heart:

Why do labels hold such power over me? Why are they so intrinsically linked to my worth? To my usefulness or importance?

Why do some labels cause me to bristle while others cause me to strut?

Whose labels affect me the most? And why?

There are labels that I pin on myself. Some are pleasant, others not so much.

There are labels that others offer me. These can be weighty. But I don't have to accept them; I get to choose which ones I wear. The choosing is not easy, but it's a snap when compared to living out the reality of my choices.

And then, there are the labels that God uses to describe me. God, the One who made me, who knows all about me. Perhaps I should choose His.

But whose labels do I really attach to my heart?

Now, it's time for the results of my self-examination. How's yours coming?

Face the truth:

Labels hold power over me because in my mind they reflect my doing. My doing reflects my performance which is linked to my worth in the world's eyes . . . okay, to be honest, sometimes even in my own eyes.

And don't we all long to be worthy? To be significant? Important? Not passed over?

"If I'm not doing enough, I'm not enough," my pride chides as he wrangles to pick the best labels.

So, we rack up the labels. The prettier sounding, the better. The longer the list, the sweeter. We gravitate towards labels that display our accomplishments, show how busy we are, or help us to fit in.

We write in, erase, check again, and often change them to match the season we're in. We are compelled to get them right. Labels define us.

When I find myself caught, once again, in a battle for my worth, I'm reminded that the labels I often choose to define my life . . . to define me . . . are my labels, their labels, but not God's.

See what great love the Father has lavished on us,
that we should be called children of God! And that
is what we are! (1 John 3:1a)

The only label that truly defines me: **Child of God.**

Not based on what I've done, what I am doing, or what I can do, but wholly on what my God has done to draw me close.

As I meditate on this label given to me by God Himself, I'm reminded that it's all about Him, not me, not me in my weakness nor me in my might.

I'm reminded to shift my focus to my God, His love, His death in my place, His indwelling presence that guides me.

I'm reminded to wear this label proudly, confidently, and with a thankful heart because He is worthy.

Great is the LORD and most worthy of praise; his greatness no one can fathom. (Psalm 145:3)

· 59 ·

Thankful.

Again, not quite the right word. But it's a start.

In this prolonged, deep-rooted war for my worth, I am so thankful for the truth that brings me victory.

What about you?

*Do labels hold more power over you than
you would like to admit?
Have you chosen labels for others that affect
how you treat them?
God's word is filled with many labels for His children.
Which one is your favorite?
Which one impacts your life the most?
Child of God: three small words, one powerful label.
Let those words sink deeply into your heart today.
Ponder them, chew on them, and live them out.*

Praise Focus: God is merciful; He calls me His child.

When Your Peace is Threatened

I KNOW GOD DOESN'T want this for me.

Especially not now.

As I prepare for Christmas, putting up the tree, making holiday plans and ordering presents, I keep trying to focus on the first Christmas, but I can't help but notice the white elephant in the room.

There he sits. Big and expensive.

And his presence is costing me big time.

I feel the tension—the unrest that springs from my ceaseless efforts to remove him, to dress him up, or simply to ignore him.

But there he sits.

Big and expensive. Staring at me. Squatting heavily on any dreams of peace I may have.

What is your white elephant?

It's okay, most of us have at least one.

I know you don't like to acknowledge it, let alone talk about it, especially at Christmas.

But bear with me. This just might be the best time to address him once and for all.

So, what is it?

Maybe it's the helplessness you feel as you watch a loved one make poor life choices, choices likely to cause harm. Your muscles tense and your stomach knots as you wait for the bomb to go off, all the while praying that God's light will shine in their darkness.

Or it could be the worry that escalates each time you glance over at the mounting bills or the uncertain job future.

Maybe it's the threat of poor health that is stealing your sense of security.

Whatever it may be—strained relationships, financial woes, health concerns, the fear of living in a world gone bad—you just can't seem to pull your eyes away from your white elephant.

Sometimes, especially at Christmas, you try to pretend he's not there. I mean, you've tried everything and he won't budge, so why not try ignoring him.

You may try to dress him up with frivolous activities and skin-deep distractions, hoping that with a disguise he won't look quite so menacing.

Yet, no matter what or how much you try, there your white elephant sits, stealthily encroaching on the peace that could be yours.

But God doesn't want this for us.

He came to bring us peace.

That first Christmas, over 2000 years ago, the angels announced peace.

Glory to God in the highest, and on earth peace, good will toward men. (Luke 2:14 KJV)

The Messiah's peace. Offered to us for all times, in various kinds of troubles and trials . . . in every situation.

And that wasn't the last we heard of this offer of peace. As God was on earth and dwelt among us through His Son, Jesus Christ, He would repeatedly remind us of this peace.

Come to me, all you who are weary and burdened, and I will give you rest. (Matthew 11:28)

Doesn't that sound wonderful? When you strain under the weight of trying to move your white elephant, doesn't rest sound refreshing?

"But," you argue, "you don't know the troubles I see." No, I don't, but Jesus knows.

I have told you these things, so that in me you will have peace. In this world you will have trouble. But take heart! I have overcome the world. (John 16:33)

Yes, He knows all the trouble we lug around and try to push out of the way.

No doubt about it, we will have trouble in this world, but Jesus says take heart!

Do not be anxious about anything, but in every situation, by prayer and petition, with thanksgiving, present your requests to God. And the peace of God, which transcends all understanding, will guard your hearts and your minds, in Christ Jesus. (Philippians 4:6-7)

There it is again—peace. The peace offered by God through the Messiah, the Christ, surpassing all human understanding, existing even in the most trying circumstances and standing guard over our minds and hearts.

Peace!

Even with the white elephant in the room.

Peace!

Even when you don't know what to do at Christmas.

Peace!

Let's revisit that invitation:

Come to me, all you who are weary and burdened, and I will give you rest. Take my yoke upon you and learn from me; for I am gentle and humble in heart, and you will find rest for your souls. (Matthew 11:28-29)

Rest for your souls ... aaaahhhh ... sounds a lot like peace to me.

So, my friend, that is my plan. To simply come to Jesus.

Fix my eyes on Him and relish the peace that He gives.

Because I know, this is what He wants for me.

What about you?

*Is your peace being threatened
by the white elephant in the room?
How are you handling that?
Are you straining on your own?
Or are you handing it over to God?*

*Praise Focus: God is love and
offers peace to His children.*

The Secret to Being at Home When You Are Not at Home

MY SON DIDN'T COME home this summer. It was his first summer away at college, so he traveled to visit friends, looked for a job, and kept himself busy spreading his budding adult wings.

I remember when I was in university thousands of miles away from home. I, too, relished my independence, but occasionally I would long for home. Like I'm yearning for home now.

It's been 11 months, and I'm still not back in my home. I'm not the only one. Many of us have been displaced by the destruction caused by Hurricane Irma and have been patiently (or not so patiently) waiting for repairs to be completed so that we can return home.

Homesickness. It's a feeling I think we can all relate to. But what exactly do we miss from home? Is it the people? Is it the place? Or is it the feeling? The assurance that you are safe and protected? Known and loved?

I've thought a lot about what home means recently and have marveled at the times I've found Home in the strangest of places and the oddest of times. Once you find Home, you never forget it.

The days following Hurricane Irma, I would rise with the dawn, make my way through the rubble, climb out through the broken door, and sit on what remained of my porch. With the roof torn off and most of the banisters gone, I had a clear view of my surroundings—the sea, the sky, and the stripped landscape. It never failed to take my breath away. But as I sat there amid the shattered, unsafe remains of my home and island, communing in silence with the sovereign God, I would find Home.

Or even during the actual hurricane, when the noise was terrifyingly loud, and fear surged through my body and threatened to overcome me, I found Home in the words of the Psalms.

There have been other times, too. Times when I struggled to let go of the reins of control or experienced deep faith-testing loss. Times when I've been struck hard by my own weaknesses. Or even when I relaxed in a season of plenty. In all of those circumstances, when life was a lot and I was longing for home, I found Home each time I retreated in silence and remembered my God.

Once you find Home, you never forget it.

It's difficult to find the words to describe Home: accepted, loved, empowered. Where compassion and mercy are the norm, life brims with possibility. You never have to doubt who you are because you know whose you are.

Home. If you haven't found Home, you'll never find rest.

So now, please join me and take some time to pause and examine where we are.

Perhaps you've found Home before, but you've drifted a bit or maybe a lot. That's okay. You're always welcomed back. Or maybe you've never found Home, but in the quiet, you long for it. Deep down, there's unrest, and you've been searching for it for a long time.

There's good news, my friend. For you and for me.

All those the Father gives me will come to me, and whoever comes to me I will never drive away. (John 6:37)

I may not be in my physical home, but I can always be at Home.

Home is not a place; it's not even a feeling. It's a Person, waiting for us to return to where we belong. He stands with open arms, offering Himself to quench the thirst deep within us.

God, it seems you've been our home forever; long before the mountains were born, Long before you brought earth itself to birth, from "once upon a time" to "kingdom come"—you are God. (Psalm 90:1-2 MSG)

There is still time to make it Home. I pray for you, for my son, for all of us to find Home, even when we are not at home; that we'll embrace the God who runs to welcome us back.

What about you?

*Is your soul at rest? Have you found Home?
Or are you still striving for peace, calm,
and rest amid the chaos?*

*Praise Focus: God is everywhere always;
He is our forever Home.*

Embracing the Hope of God in Loss

But this I call to mind, and therefore I have **hope***: The steadfast love of the Lord never ceases; his mercies never come to an end; they are new every morning; great is your faithfulness. (Lamentations 3:21-23)*

May the God of **hope** *fill you with all joy and peace in believing, so that by the power of the Holy Spirit you may abound in* **hope***. (Romans 15:13)*

Is There Hope for the One Who Suffers Alone?

THESE LAST FEW DAYS have been filled with hope.

A hope that started out full and expectant, but day by agonizing day, moment by heart-rending moment, dwindled away.

Down to a sliver, a tiny thread of a spider web, but still, we desperately clung on, hoping against hope that our hearts' desire would miraculously materialize.

Hoping until all hope was gone.

Or so it seemed.

At moments like these, I retreat inside. Crawl up and hide. Alone. Alone with my pain, my suffering, my unanswerable questions.

Have you ever been there?

Racked by an unexpected pain; one that is hot and searing and burns you to the core? A pain that is personal and deep.

Maybe you can relate. Maybe you've been there. And maybe you were alone in your suffering.

But in my loneliness, way down deep in the depths of me, I meet Hope.

Not the hope of this world that disappoints.

A Hope that picks me up and carries me at the very lowest and saddest times of my life. A Hope that promises never to leave me or forsake me.

A promise I can rely upon, even in my darkest moments.

"I have told you all this so that you may have peace in me. Here on earth you will have many trials and sorrows. But take heart, because I have overcome the world." (John 16:33 NLT)

My heart breaks. I think of my loss.

And then I think of those who have no Hope, who suffer alone. I pray that they would know that it doesn't have to be that way.

My heart swells and aches with raw emotion. Pain, suffering, but in the midst . . . **hope** and gratitude.

Gratitude for God's unconditional, never-ending love for us.

A love that is relentless in His pursuit of us.

A love that is not earned but gifted.

A love that knows no bounds and can never be defeated. **Never.**

And I am convinced that nothing can ever separate us from God's love. Neither death nor life, neither angels nor demons, neither our fears for today nor our worries about tomorrow—not even the powers of hell can separate us from God's love. No power in the sky above or in the earth below—indeed, nothing in all creation will ever be able to separate us from the love of God that is revealed in Christ Jesus our Lord. (Romans 8: 38-39 NLT)

A love that beckons us to come just as we are, alone and suffering, to accept His gift. The gift of His presence with us.

A Presence that embraces us, lifts us up, comforts us, empowers us, transforms us.

A Presence that, God, in his mercy, assured me my dear brother felt and embraced. A presence that gets me through the storm.

A presence that I am eternally grateful for.

My friend, when it comes down to it, when everything else is stripped away, the only thing that matters and that has any eternal significance is that we understand and experience the **love of Christ for us**.

So, as I sit in my suffering, lovingly nestled in the arms of my Father, I pray for you: the one who suffers alone. I pray that you may have the power to understand, as all God's people should, *how wide, how long, how high, and how deep his love is (Ephesians 3:18 NLT)*. That you may place your trust in Him—the only Hope that endures—so that you never, ever have to suffer alone again.

What about you?

Have you been there? Feeling lonely?
Believing that you are alone?
In desperate need of hope?
You are never alone; God never abandons us and
promises to always hold us close.
Have you experienced this hope?

Praise Focus: God is here with us
even when we feel alone.

How to Find Peace When Life Feels Abnormal

FEAR. IT SEEMS LIKE he's always there lurking in the shadows, waiting to pounce on me.

At times he jumps out at me suddenly, knocking me right off my feet, screaming a spine-chilling word—abnormal! Other times, he stealthily and cunningly sneaks up on me, until we are walking hand in hand.

Then he whispers poison in my ears.

"Abnormal," he spoke into the gaping hole of sadness and grief when I lost my father.

"Abnormal," he screamed into the absence, panic, and searing pain when my youngest brother, a seasoned seaman, was lost at sea.

"Abnormal," he confirmed when I emerged from my refuge, observing the devastation to my home and community in the wake of Hurricane Irma.

I had become familiar with Fear's favorite word, spoken especially for me.

So, when Fear invited himself along to drop off my firstborn at college (a year earlier than originally planned), it was no surprise when he tried the word again, behind each of my steps, "Abnormal. Abnormal. Abnormal."

But here is the thing that Fear never counts on . . . within the abnormal, there is a *still, small voice* (*1 Kings 19:12 KJV*) soothing my weary, anxious soul.

The voice declares, "I am here."

And just like that, I sense the normal that remains with me when life feels abnormal. It's in the comfort and hope I find when God calls me to retreat in a quiet place with Him. He reminds me of His love, His faithfulness, and His sovereignty. He assures me that He will never change and that His love for me lasts forever.

The amazing paradox of it all is that my God is **not normal**! Not even in the slightest!

He is not average or regular or usual. He is above all (*Psalm 97:9 ESV*).

Period.

He can do exceedingly more than we ask or even imagine (*Ephesians 3:20.*)

He never changes (*James 1:17*), and He promises to always be my Normal through all my abnormal seasons of life.

No matter how insistently Fear stomps his feet, shouting "abnormal," no matter how enticingly he tries to draw me in, seductively calling me to hide in the shadows with him. . . I can refuse.

I can choose to stand in the light of my Normal: His presence, His power, His protection, and provision.

Fear encourages me to run, fight, and strive with all of my might; to put things back the way they're supposed to be.

But instead, I choose to stand in the armor of my Normal and remember Who it is that fights for me.

So, when I'm in the midst of another bout of abnormal, I cling to my God and He leads me to a place that I can't explain. A place where fear is defeated and peace abounds. Peace that is anything but normal. Peace that lifts me up and carries me through the abnormal.

I pray that same peace for you, no matter what Fear may be whispering into your heart.

What about you?

Has your normal been knocked from under you?
Are you praying for life to settle down?
To feel normal again?
Reach out to our God who never changes, who is the
same yesterday and today and forever (Hebrews 13:8)
and find your rest in Him.

Praise Focus: God never changes and
promises never to leave us.

Does Time Have You in a Choke Hold?

THE PAIN BUBBLES UP and spills over, as hot, salty tears run down my cheeks.

The fact that I hurt so deeply for someone I've never met doesn't even surprise me.

The twinges of sorrow have been seething under the surface for some time now, waiting to overflow.

I peer at her bright smiling face and feel it again—the aching, the longing, the wrestling with time.

If only one could turn back time.

Pain. It stands at the edge of our not-perfect-but-we-love-them lives and claws and tears with its sinister talons.

No one is left unscathed.

We struggle, we writhe, we squirm, trying desperately to escape its grasp, to return to the time when pain was not.

Have you ever felt that? The overwhelming almost urgent desire to turn back the hands of time, just change that one tiny thing that caused our world to come crashing down on us.

We know it is impossible, but oh, how we wish we could.

It was just a mistake, a foolish choice. Who could know it would end up like this?

And so, we struggle.

Sometimes, I feel like I'm caught in a battle with time. He's the one who has the upper hand and who has me in a choke hold.

Can you relate?

Looking back and wishing you could change the past does nothing but fill you with despair and regret.

Not exactly the components of living a victorious life.

You try to pull yourself together. Waiting for time to soften the blow, you shift your focus and peer longingly into the future.

But even here, my friend, we must be careful. Fixating on the future often leaves us unhappy with today, unable to enjoy the essence of now.

You know us moms, sometimes we get so caught up in preparing our kids for the future that we forget to slow down and enjoy today.

Or we look longingly to the day when we can . . . _________________________. You fill in the blanks. We all have something that tries to hijack our promise of joy for today.

So, what's a girl to do?

I'm starting to realize that our big picture view of life has a lot to do with how we envision time and, likewise, the way we understand time greatly impacts how we feel about our lives.

Are we at the mercy of time? Or is time just a tool in the hands of our Master?

When we are locked in the battle with time, tossed between languishing over the past or yearning for the future, between the "if onlys" and the "one days," we can find hope in turning to the only One who sits outside of time and sees it all.

We can turn to God, our Father in heaven.

Give Him Our Yesterdays

Forget the former things; do not dwell on the past. See, I am doing a new thing! Now it springs up; do you not perceive it? I am making a way in the wilderness and streams in the wasteland. (Isaiah 43:18-19)

"But you don't understand, it is so painful," you say.

God says, "I am making a way!"

I am so grateful that God's mercies are *new every morning (Lamentations 3:23 ESV)*. He is always at work doing a new thing, making a way in the wilderness that is life. Are we looking for it? Are our eyes opened to what He is doing now? Or are they straining to see yesterday?

"But you don't know what I've done," you say. But God says, "For I will forgive their wickedness and will remember their sins no more" (Hebrews 8:12).

Can you imagine such grace? Once you have accepted God's offer of forgiveness, let the past go;

God has. Don't let your yesterday's mistakes rob you of the joy of today.

He Holds Our Tomorrows

As for your future, leave it in His hands. He's already there anyway.

"But I am trusting you O LORD, saying, 'You are my God!' My future is in your hands" (Psalm 31:14-15a NLT).

No, we don't have to worry about the future when we are walking with God, but we still do. We are so entangled by our strife with time that we forget that no matter what happens, His presence never leaves us, and our eternal future is secure with Him.

Nor should we boast about the future.

Now listen, you who say, "Today or tomorrow we will go to this or that city, spend a year there, carry on business and make money." Why, you do not even know what will happen tomorrow. What is your life? You are a mist that appears for a little while and then vanishes. Instead, you ought to say, "If it is the Lord's will, we will live and do this or that." (James 4:13-15)

So, if we can neither change the past nor fast-forward to the future, shouldn't we make the best of now?

Live for Him Today

Easier said than done, but it's time. Time to stop battling with time and be free from its stranglehold. Let's purposely and prayerfully take our gaze off time and peer instead on our omnipotent Father in heaven—the only all-powerful One who is the same yesterday, today and tomorrow. He forgives our yesterdays and secures our tomorrows, standing at the door, knocking, and calling emphatically . . . "Today."

"At just the right time, I heard you. On the day of salvation, I helped you." Indeed the "right time" is now. Today is the day of salvation. (2 Corinthians 6:2 NLT)

Today if you hear his voice do not harden your hearts. (Hebrews 3:15)

He calls us to a life of hope, a life of joy in His presence . . . of peace beyond understanding and of love incomprehensible.

Not an easy life, necessarily; there will still be pockmarks of pain and distress, but our view of time changes when we are cradled in the arms of the One who created time. We live to make the best use of our time for Him. And as we love . . . love those left behind and marred by pain, we shine brightly for Him in the dark shadows of life.

I pray that God, in His mercy, would *teach us to realize the brevity of life so that we may grow in wisdom (Psalm 90:12 NLT)* and that we would embrace the freedom He offers to live fully, abundantly, right now, right where we are . . . in joy . . . in love . . . in Him.

What about you?

Do you battle with time?
Is your fixation with time stealing your joy today?

Praise Focus: God is eternal and is not limited by time.

How to Find Joy When Your Heart Isn't Quiet

May the God of hope fill you with all joy and peace in believing, so that by the power of the Holy Spirit you may abound in hope. (Romans 15:13 ESV)

Silence can be complicated.

There's the silence that is found when a mom gazes into the eyes of her newborn baby . . . or when lovers linger long in each other's eyes.

A pleasant, heart-warming silence.

But then, there's the other silence.

The silence of fear accompanied only by the clippety-clop of your galloping heart.

Or the eerie silence that is heard in the dead center of a fierce storm.

Yep, silence is tricky. Sometimes a friend, sometimes a foe.

And sometimes it's just on the surface.

You know that kind. The one that sparkles and shines while proudly stating that all is well with you.

The one that others see, that sometimes even you believe is real.

But deep down in your heart, it is not quiet. The truth screams to you: this silence is just a farce.

Discomfited by the disharmony, your spirit longs for more. When there's no quiet within, no matter how calm and bright it looks on the outside, you can't be content, happy, free of cares, joyous . . . you get the point.

Joy. My one word for 2017.

This year as I trudged along amidst the ups and downs, I tried to focus on joy, an even-keeled joy that remains through tears and smiles. By God's grace, I came to realize that that kind of joy comes only by surrender, by forgetting who

I am and bowing down before the King of this world.

But the silence of surrender is not always quiet.

Sometimes, it is accompanied by striving; an unrest that says, "I'm still not sure I can trust you." A desire to hold onto control . . . a not-fully-letting-go type of surrender. Perhaps in some way a failure to fully grasp the peace that was offered that first Christmas.

A few years ago, I broke with tradition and put up a white Christmas tree. I've never been a fan of white Christmas trees, but that year I felt drawn to one. The color—a sign of surrender—was symbolic to me. All decked out in apple green and turquoise with pastel lights, my tree twinkled and glowed beautifully. To crown it all, I printed out, colored and pasted on my walls these words: peace, joy, hope, and love. It was perfect. Despite the gentle prodding from my husband, those words remained on my walls for years.

As I lived out my messy life, my eyes would be drawn to those words as ever-present reminders of the fruits of surrender.

But following Hurricane Irma a couple of months ago, I found the pieces of those same words strewn across my ravaged home. I wondered, "How quiet is my surrender? Will I accept good and not bad from my Father? Or will I be at ease, content even when . . . ?"

As I held the ragged scraps of paper, tears streamed down my face. I pondered those four words and their inextricable link. Could I experience joy, hope, peace, and love in the silence of my night? Am I like a *weaned child with its mother* (Psalm 131:2), trusting God to provide as He sees fit? Is my spirit quieted and calmed despite the turmoil? Am I able to enjoy God's gifts even in the mess?

Experiencing joy in the unrest has been a challenge for me.

But I'm learning, dear friends, about the link between quiet and joy. About the quiet that shatters my silence, strips away my need for control, and shushes the noisiness of my doubts. The quiet that wraps me in the assurance of a Love that knows no bounds—a deep, personal love, beautifully displayed in my Saviour's humble birth, His sacrificial death in my place, and His unending desire for my good.

The kind of quiet that seeps deep within and hushes my restless heart.

Those words jump off the littered floor and into my heart.

The striving stops.

Peace flows, hope abounds, love is shared, and joy spills over.

It is the even-keeled joy that I longed to keep not just at Christmas, but all year long. Even among my falling tears, this joy, rooted in love and intertwined with hope and peace makes silence my friend. Because deep down in my heart, I know, without a shadow of a doubt, that it is well with my soul.

Joy.

My prayer for you, dear friend, is that in your silent night, you'll look up and see the God who knows our imperfect, noisy surrender, our shaky desire to bow down, and still showers us with His love. That you'll allow His love to break into your silence, quiet the unrest within, and spill over as joy.

A joy that lasts the whole year through.

What about you?

Do you abound in hope despite the noisiness of life?
Is your happiness just on the surface?
Or have you found deep-seated joy?
Let's dig a little deeper:
Have you found peace in believing,
or do you struggle to surrender?

Praise Focus: God is good.
He offers us peace and joy.

What I Need to Remember When My Shoulders Ache

We are troubled on every side, yet not distressed; we are perplexed, but not in despair; Persecuted, but not forsaken; cast down, but not destroyed. (2 Corinthians 4:8-9 KJV)

THE DARK, HEAVY CLOUDS hang low, trying their utmost to block out the rays of life-giving sun.

The spiny, gnarled branches of broken trees claw at me like bony fingers digging and scraping at any remaining hope.

Brokenness. Life struggling to break through. The evidence is all around.

I live in a post-disaster zone.

Most days, I'm fine. I hold my head up and keep moving on step-by-purposeful-step.

Other days I feel it—the pressing down, the throbbing soreness.

But it's not because of the environment.

Yes, I suppose that contributes. Perhaps it heightens my senses, makes me more aware of the broken, disfigured world we live in, and more in tune with the hurt all around me.

You see, everywhere I look there's always something to remind me.

People are struggling. Life is hard.

There's the obvious—the diagnoses, the senseless violence, the families torn apart—raw, exposed sores of pain, out in the open; stories too hard to hear.

There's also an oppressive ache, the one that no one shouts from rooftops, but if you keep your ear to the ground, you'll feel it.

It's the deep, gnawing heartache of living in a world that was never intended to be this way.

Everyone is carrying a heavy burden.

That's when my shoulders start to ache.

I get quiet and retreat inside. Looking for answers.

I feel their burdens. I feel their hopelessness . . . their never-ending search for peace and happiness.

I feel the guilt. "I need to pray more," I scold myself. There's just so much need.

The knots tighten.

I sit quietly under the dark cloud.

And then . . .

The light breaks through. As it always does.

Thank God, my God is a Big God.

The truth brings me clarity.

Yes, He can handle it all. The burdens may be numerous, but He is able and willing to lift them all.

As I sit there with Him, He reassures me. He sees it all. He knows it all. And He cares.

Words are not needed. We commune in silence.

I lay the burdens on His shoulders. He picks them up and carries each one.

Sometimes, I whisper a name. He knows instantly who I'm talking about. He knows just what they need.

He listens. He acts.

And I rest my head on His shoulders as His personal and powerful promises pour over me.

The darkness, the brokenness will not win.

I remember this.

When my heart bleeds, and my shoulders ache from burdens brought on by living in the already-but-not-yet, striving to survive in the tumultuous times of a world gone bad, I remember . . .

My shoulders will never be big enough to carry this world's burdens. My prayers will always feel like a drop in the bucket. I will never be able to do enough, but my God can.

He has promised to lift the burdens that I can't carry.

So, I'm holding Him to His promise. I'm handing them over to Him. He is a big God. Not only is He able, but He longs to help us.

Will you join me in handing over your shoulder-aching baggage?

I feel the tension ease away. Don't you?

Peace begins to trickle in. My God's got this.

These things I have spoken unto you, that in me ye might have peace. In the world ye shall have tribulation: but be of good cheer; I have overcome the world. (John 16:33 KJV)

Come unto me, all ye that labor and are heavy laden, and I will give you rest. (Matthew 11:28)

And God shall wipe away all tears from their eyes; and there shall be no more death, neither sorrow, nor crying, neither shall there be any more pain: for the former things are passed away. (Revelation 21:4 KJV)

What about you?

What is making your shoulders ache today?
Have you been so focused on the struggles of this life
that you've forgotten how big your God is?

Praise Focus: God is sovereign and infinitely rich in
power, compassion, mercy, and grace.

When You're in a Desperate Search for Safety

As I peered over the edge of the dinghy, I could feel the fear surging up in me.

They told me it was the best fishing spot, but all I could see was the wreck way down below. There it lay silent, yet menacing, a constant reminder that someone before me had failed to sense the danger of this deceivingly calm spot. As an innately fearful child who couldn't swim, sitting in a tiny vessel in the middle of the deep untamed ocean was hardly my favorite place to be.

But, although my insides screamed, "Get me out of here," I took a deep breath, held on tightly to the seat, and tried my best to remain calm.

Perhaps because I knew that even though I could potentially fall overboard, sink to the depths of the sea and be lost forever (and yes that's exactly how I imagined it), I also knew that my dad and older brother would do anything to protect me. Their very presence, right next to me in the boat, made me feel safe.

Safe in the presence of danger.

What makes you feel safe?

I've been thinking a lot about safety recently.

Perhaps it's having been touched by unexpected, searing loss and change, while feeling the need to run. Maybe it's just watching the news or reading the headlines in a world that seems intent on self-destruction. It could be feeling helpless in the spate of natural disasters that seems to be stalking us. Or simply, it's the mom instinct in me that knows no limits when it comes to keeping my children safe.

Or perhaps it's a combination of all. Whatever it may be, it has brought safety front and center in my mind.

As I reminisce on those childhood fishing trips, I'm reminded that we get to choose which 'fishermen' we could have in the boat with us. You know those persons (places, things or ideas) that we surround ourselves with that may not necessarily cancel out the danger, but somehow make us feel safe.

We get to choose them.

Maybe, for you, it's the well-paying job, the two-story home in the nice neighborhood, the lump sum in the bank, and the retirement plan that help you sleep at night. Maybe it's the car you drive and the friends you keep. Or it's the idea that if you work hard and plan well you should get by without too much of a scrape. Perhaps it's a clean bill of health on your last medical check-up. Or your skill set along with the decisions that you make that, in your opinion, set you apart from other people. Or maybe it's just your pattern of normal—the predictability of the usual—that makes you feel safe.

We each have our own unique combination—a precarious balance between the pursuit of safety and the presence of danger.

But sometimes, so drawn are we to it that, without even realizing it, safety becomes an idol in our lives. We fall prey to its sweet seduction. It's as if we'd rather have safe than have God.

So, my friend, I pause now and ask you, "Which fishermen have you chosen? Who or what do you pursue with your whole being in your unending quest for safe?"

Just like in my childhood fishing trips, I know the choice matters. Choosing my dad and brother, both experienced fishermen with the desire, ability, and skill to protect me, was a wise choice. Choosing my sister, one even more terrified of the wreck than me and without the skill or ability to save me, would have been a very foolish choice.

I'm looking intently at all my foolish choices right now, and I'm rediscovering the only wise choice.

You see, despite all the chaos surrounding me, I just can't shake this feeling that I have: there's only one Fisherman that can really keep me safe—my Father in heaven.

That is the anchor of truth that keeps me safe in the presence of ubiquitous danger.

"I have this hope in the depth of my soul. In the flood or the fire, you're with me and You won't let go!"[9]

It's a hope I wish to share because I know that I'm not the only one whose in a desperate search for safety.

So, I'm leaving you with a few key verses that I've been meditating on. Verses that remind me of God's plan for my eternal safety. Verses that sprout like green leaves after the storm and replenish my hope with the promise of life.

I pray these refreshing verses will help to steer us as we choose which fisherman sits in the boat with us and that our choice will be one that ensures our eternal safety.

Salvation is found in no one else; for there is no other name under heaven given to mankind by which we must be saved. (Acts 4:12)

Fear of man will prove to be a snare, but whoever trusts in the LORD is kept safe. (Proverbs 29:25)

The name of the Lord is a fortified tower; the righteous run to it and are safe. (Proverbs 18:10)

The Lord will rescue me from every evil attack and will bring me safely to his heavenly kingdom. To him be glory for ever and ever. Amen. (2 Timothy 4: 18)

What about you?

What makes you feel safe?
Has safety become an idol in your life?
Are you trusting in Christ alone for your eternal safety?

Praise Focus: God is all-powerful;
His children are safe in His hands.

Beyond the Storms, A Spark of Hope

"Be strong and courageous. Do not be afraid or terrified because of them, for the LORD your God goes with you; he will never leave you nor forsake you." (Deut. 31:6)

REELING IN SHOCK. THAT'S how I would describe our small community after a series of senseless murders and fatal accidents claimed the lives of several of our young men. In a community as connected as ours, the tragedies always come too close to home. We are all affected. This flood of unfortunate events was so sudden, so tragic that some started to suspect the work of unnatural forces. In a community familiar with hurricanes, this kind of storm blew us off of our feet as dark clouds of pain and fear settled on our small islands.

These tragedies came on the heel of two major losses in my family: one somewhat expected and another that only exists in nightmares. Losing both my father and my youngest brother within a short period rocked me to the core—the pain hot and real and lasting.

On the world stage, things were no better. We need only look to our closest neighbor to see the waves of uneasiness—rising tensions, riots, and protests that follow an unpredicted election result scream, "Uncertain times!" Wars and rumors of wars, refugees, terrorist attacks, corruption, and greed dominate global media coverage. Without a doubt, these are grim times.

To say that hope was struggling to breathe would be an understatement.

I had read about God's promise of joy and his admonition to *count it all joy (James 1:12 KJV)*, but in reality, joy seemed missing in action, drowning under the turbulent seas of life.

I wondered about my children. I wondered what they felt deep down about all of these things.

I understood in a fresh way the delusional need of our youth to sedate themselves with a continuous stream of entertainment. Living for what makes one happy does seem to offer a respite from all that ails us, but I wondered about the questions that float through their minds in their infrequent moments of quiet and being unplugged.

I wondered if a steady, unwavering joy and hope that steers us on were within their grasp.

And so I grabbed them by their hands, walked to the edge of our crazy circumstances and dove right into the book of Revelation.

Revelation? Really?

Really!

I recall my childhood memories of Revelation were not too pretty: fire and brimstone, the moon turning to blood, stars falling from the skies. What was I thinking? What twisted love is this? Did I plan for them to be scared to death or coerced by fear?

No; I was simply diving down in search of hope . . . a hope grounded in love that leads to joy . . . hope that changes the lens through which we view the events of our time. Hope that gives meaning to today and assurance for tomorrow.

These times were too perilous to leave my children drifting on the rickety boat of their own making. They needed to see Christ as our Captain.

Together we would sail the seas and, together, we would search.

It started out with smooth sailing. The introduction brims with hope; the letters to the churches are relevant, convicting, and encouraging. Yep, those first few chapters of Revelation are bursting with the promise of reward.

But soon, we sailed into choppy waters. One morning, as I was pre-reading the upcoming chapters, I felt the old fears of my childhood memories bobbing to the surface. The images were downright creepy—even for me. I could only imagine my children's reactions.

In a moment of doubt, I thought maybe this was not such a good idea after all. Maybe we'll just read something different, something more hope-inspiring.

But I kept reading on. This was, after all, the revelation of Jesus Christ. Jesus Christ revealing

Himself to us; I needed to see more. My children needed to see more—more of Him.

Besides, a blessing was promised to everyone who reads it: *God blesses the one who reads the words of this prophecy to the church, and he blesses all who listen to its message and obey what it says, for the time is near.* (Revelation 1:3 NLT)

So, I pushed past the images of the apocalypse to see Jesus. And I decided to start with the end.

Sometimes, I think if we can know how the story ends, the scary twists and turns of the plot won't seem so intimidating after all. A spoiler for sure, but hey, in this life, I think we all could benefit from a spoiler like this one.

So, I leaned in close to my Captain, braced myself against His strength, and prayerfully steered my children's gaze straight to the end of the story. Right then and there, I skipped right over the hairy parts that seem ghoulish in detail and read the final few chapters of Revelation for them.

Ahh! Somehow just reading those passages strengthens my sea legs. When I meditate on His rock-solid promises, I don't feel so tossed about anymore. I know life is rough and will continue to be rough. I shudder when I think of all the possibilities. But I also know that I have a Captain who promises to never leave me nor forsake me *(Hebrews 13:5)* and assures me of safe passage.

As I cling to this mast of hope, I fix my gaze at the rising joy that leads me deeper into Him. And He steels me for the onward journey.

As for my children, thankfully, I don't need to rely on my imperfect navigation skills and my flawed understanding of the course. God has promised a guide for our journey—His Holy Spirit—and He will lead us into all truth. On Him, we can depend.

Yes, the journey is not over. Together, my children and I would continue our search through the book of Revelation and though the tempests rage, we would drop anchor at all the choppy parts in the full hope of uncovering what treasures lie beneath. I think we are in for quite an adventure!

May God bless you as you travel on.

What about you?

Where do you find hope?
What are your thoughts about the book of Revelation?
Love? Fear? Avoidance? Confusion? Or blessing?

Praise Focus: God is eternal;
He knows the end from the beginning.

Are You Missing God's Big Plan for Your Life?

"How do you know? You can't know that for sure."

The words from my son came clear and crisp, right on the heel of my declaring a blessing: "The Lord has big plans for you."

Coming from one who doesn't often have much to say, the words took me by surprise.

Perhaps if I weren't a mother, I would learn it a different way and master the lesson God has been desperately trying to teach me.

But I am convinced that God is using my children, the ones he chose specifically for me, to mold me and shape me, to chisel away the dross that keeps building up, to reveal His truth to me, and to make me more like him.

The hardest lessons come through my mistakes—but those have been the best.

Have you ever made the mistake of implying to others that God's big plan of grace isn't enough? That what he has planned for them is more important than *Who* he has planned for them? That somehow, there is something that God needs for them to do?

Perhaps you haven't. Perhaps you have always relayed the truth of the gospel in its glorious, beautiful simplicity. No additions. No conditions. No traditions. Nothing but the gospel; nothing but the reason Christ came.

For God so loved the world, that he gave his only Son, that whoever believes in him should not perish but have eternal life. (John 3:16 ESV)

Truly, truly, I say to you, whoever hears my word and believes him who sent me has eternal life. He does not come into judgement but has passed from death to life. (John 5:24 ESV)

As I sat there pondering my son's words, I climbed behind his eyes for a bit and tried to see things the way he did.

Within the last few months, he had lost his young, carefree, fun-loving uncle who, by the world's standard, had not yet found God's big plan for his life. He had also lost his I'm-on-the-verge-of-*my*-life soccer mate, who was just 19 when he 'missed out' on God's big plan for his life.

And now here I am telling him that God has big plans for his life.

Really?

And with those four simple words—how do you know—the chiseling began.

What is God's big plan for our lives? How do we know what His plan is?

I think, perhaps, God likes to play connect-the-dots with me. I'm just not always good at the game. He keeps saying . . . look closely and you'll see . . . the picture will slowly come into focus. One day, one glorious morning, you will see the big picture of my will.

*For this is the will of my Father, that everyone
who looks on the Son and believes in him should*

have eternal life, and I will raise him up on the last day. (John 6:40 ESV)

Looking at life from my son's perspective reminded me of another conversation with my youngest brother.

A week before he went missing at sea, God blessed me with a wonderful gift—an unplanned conversation that gave me a glimpse into my brother's awareness of God in his life.

As I listened to him, I had said, "Carlos, God is relentlessly pursuing you. It's up to you now to . . ."

And then I paused . . . to do what?

- Get your life together?
- Start living for God?
- Go to church?
- ???

The list goes on.

What were my good intentions and well wishes for my brother's future adding to the gospel? Sometimes without realizing it, we become stumbling blocks in front of the grace and mercy Jesus offers.

My brother didn't need anything else. We don't need anything else.

In a week, my brother was gone, and in my grief I had accused God of not giving him a chance.

But he did have a chance. A chance to believe.

God simply wants me to believe.

Believe that before I was even born, he knew me . . . knew I would wander from Him.

Believe He has a plan, a plan to bring me back to Him.

Believe that this plan is achieved through Christ living a righteous life, a life that I could never live, willingly suffering the punishment I deserve for my willful rebellion and offering me His clean slate.

Believe that I'm forgiven, justified, and brought back to God, to know Him—my treasure and my joy—all through what Christ did for me.

Believe that God's big plan for my life is simply to know Him.

And that is enough!

Oh, my friend, sometimes we spend so much time waiting for God's big plan to unfold in our lives . . . in our children's lives . . . in the lives of our loved ones . . . convincing ourselves that God has something for us to do for Him.

But what if . . .

What if we're sending the wrong message? Inadvertently painting a misguided picture of God's plan for our lives, like it must show up in a big, visible way or else we're missing out. What if we keep missing it because we're looking in the wrong place?

What if God's big plan for our lives is simply to receive His offer of grace?

Then they said to him, "What must we do, to be doing the works of God?" Jesus answered them, "This is the work of God, that you believe in him whom he has sent." (John 6:28-29 ESV)

And this is eternal life, that they know you, the only true God, and Jesus Christ whom you have sent. (John 17:3 ESV)

"For I know the plans I have for you," declares the LORD, "plans to prosper you and not to harm you, plans to give you hope and a future. (Jeremiah 29:11)

I love that verse—a verse about God's plans for me. (I also think it just may be one of the most misquoted verses of all time.)

The more I connect the dots, the more I realize that on this side of eternity, not everyone will be a king, but everyone can know the King. And that, my friend, is huge. Bigger than any plan *you* can envision. It's a big, shining ball of hope that promises an eternal future with Him!

That night, talking to my brother, I had stumbled over my words. Eventually, I landed on this one simple, yet profound, word: respond.

"Carlos, God is pursuing you with His relentless love . . . you simply have to respond."

But these are written so that you may believe that Jesus is the Christ, the Son of God, and that by believing you may have life in his name .(John 20:31 ESV)

Because, if you confess with your mouth that Jesus is Lord and believe in your heart that God raised him from the dead, you will be saved. For with the heart one believes and is justified, and with the mouth one confesses and is saved. For the Scripture says, "Everyone who believes in him will not be put to shame." (Romans 10:9-11 ESV)

Often when we celebrate my brother's life, I choose to listen to songs he shared with me. They are songs of redemption that allowed him to sense anew God's closeness to him. He struggled to describe it.

I am overcome by emotion each time I listen to these songs, but I'm grateful to a God who helps me connect the dots. Grateful that He mercifully gave me a glimpse of my brother's response. Grateful for His love and mercy that reaches out and says, "Trust my plan . . . my big plan for you, my plan to bring you back to me."

Yes, I am grateful for each new breath that draws me deeper into Him, each new opportunity to share His message of hope with you, with my children, with all of those who are still desperately searching for God's big plan for their lives.

I am grateful that I can say, "Yes, my son, I am sure. God does have a big plan for you!"

What about you?

Do you believe God has a big plan for your life?
What exactly does that look like?
Big dreams? World stage? Beauty in the trenches?
A heart that reflects Him?
Today, why not spend some time considering what
God has said about the plans He has for you.

Praise Focus: God is Sovereign and All-knowing;
He knew us before we were even born.

Will There Really Be a Morning?

NIGHTS WERE HARDER FOR my mom. Perhaps the encroaching darkness worked to heighten her fears to a frenzy and strangle out the little hope she held on to.

But for me, the mornings were the worst.

Mornings, with their bright sunshine heralding in a new day, are supposed to bring fresh hope, good news, and relief. But each morning, I would dread opening my eyes as the harsh reality sank in.

In the days following the tragedy, I remember trying to catch up with my *Open My Eyes November Scripture Writing Plan*,[10] a focus on Thanksgiving & Gratitude, no less. I would read the scripture, highlight it in my *You Version*[11] Bible app and meditate on it as I carefully wrote it out in my journal. But when I came upon Psalm 30, I struggled.

> *You turned my wailing into dancing; you removed my sackcloth and clothed me with joy, that my heart may sing your praises and not be silent. LORD, my God, I will praise you forever. (Psalm 30:11-12)*

And that wasn't all. As I read more of the Psalm, I found this . . .

> *Weeping may stay for the night but rejoicing comes in the morning. (Psalm 30:5)*

Yep, I knew about the weeping, but the rejoicing? I couldn't envision it yet.

All I could think at that time was, "Will there really be a morning?"

Perhaps, you've been there. Perhaps you are there. Going through some trial in your life, something unexpected, something you'd rather not have to go through, and you're wondering will it ever really end. Will you ever feel joy again?

For days, I refused to highlight the passage, let alone write it out. But I kept coming back to it. I knew in my heart that I could trust God . . . that despite my feelings, there really would be a morning. A time when I could once again look upon the mercies of my Lord, new every morning, and rejoice.

Somewhat reluctantly, I highlighted the verse and thoughtfully wrote it out.

Then, I trusted God and waited.

And as I waited, I prayed.

I prayed for my mom, my family, for all those God laid upon my heart. I prayed that we would be comforted by His presence through the watches of the night, and that we would once again see the beauty of the mornings.

I thought about the patriarchs of the Bible who would rise early to meet with God. Even Jesus. Then I noticed something. In good times and in tough times, God was always there. I started to see more clearly—**Life is hard, but God is here**. When we meditate on the truths of His word and lean into His presence, we catch glimpses of that morning when all will be well.

God, in His mercy, has filled His Word with morning messages that swell with hope. He knows how much we need to find solace in His promises of a new day to come.

Let the morning bring me word of your unfailing love, for I have put my trust in you. Show me the way I should go, for to you I entrust my life. (Psalm 143:8)

In the morning, LORD, you hear my voice; in the morning I lay my requests before you and wait expectantly. (Psalm 5:3)

But I will sing of your strength, in the morning I will sing of your love; for you are my fortress, my refuge in times of trouble. (Psalm 59:16)

Satisfy us in the morning with your unfailing love, that we may sing for joy and be glad all our days. (Psalm 90:14)

Because of the LORD's great love, we are not consumed, for his compassions never fail. They are new every morning; great is your faithfulness. (Lamentations 3:22-23)

I wait for the Lord more than watchmen wait for the morning, more than watchmen wait for the morning. (Psalm 130:6)

He wakens me morning by morning, wakens my ear to listen like one being instructed. (Isaiah 50:4b)

These mornings, I'm rising early, and I'm meeting with my God. I'm finding more and more reasons to rejoice in His word and in His world.

In an answer to my prayer, my mom has started taking photos again and is peeking through the pain to find the beauty of the mornings once again.

My friend, I know right now you may be experiencing nighttime and a slew of dark circumstances that you just can't seem to shake. But God's love is unshakable and His presence never leaves us. Take heart, be of good courage, and lean into Him; there will be a morning.

Perhaps you've caught sight of it already, and the hope of it keeps you going. Why not share that hope with someone today? Someone who desperately needs to believe that *weeping may stay for the night, but rejoicing comes in the morning (Psalm 30:5).*

Even though we may only grasp snippets of that bright, sunshiny joy on our journey here below, God has made a promise. One glorious day, He will come again and in *the light of His presence, it will always be morning (Revelation 22:5).*

Now, isn't that something to look forward to?

What about you?

*Do you desperately long for the morning? Feel
entrapped by the dark night of life?
Have you found hope in God's promise that
morning is coming?
Lift your head, my friend, pray to the
Lord of mornings, and wait for His perfect timing.
Morning will come.*

*Praise Focus: God is faithful;
He always keeps His promises.*

How Has Empty Impacted Your Life?

The thief comes only to steal and kill and destroy; I have come that they may have life, and have it to the full. (John 10:10)

IF YOU KNOW ME personally, you'll know that I'm not a wear-your-heart-on-your-sleeve kind of girl.

Neither am I one who cries often.

But empty has a way of breaking a girl down.

Empty.

You can hardly hear the word without wincing.

If you've ever been touched by empty, you'll understand.

It seems like pain and empty walk hand in hand.

Perhaps it's because life is just not meant to be that way.

It's not meant to be empty.

Now the earth was formless and empty, darkness was over the surface of the deep, and the Spirit of God was hovering over the waters. (Genesis 1:2)

God saw all that he had made, and behold, it was very good. (Genesis 1:31)

Empty is unnatural, abnormal, and foreign.

It's painful stripping never leaves us the way it met us.

Looking back, I remember the tears that poured each time I was visited by empty.

When I saw my father's empty, vacant body, I cried.

When the boat returned empty, devoid of life, I cried.

When I stared at the empty, barren landscape, I cried.

There were more, but I don't need to go on. I'm sure you have your own.

Times when you have looked up and found empty staring right back at you. When you've tucked your tail between your legs and retreated in fear and silence.

Or perhaps empty is the way you feel inside, and no matter how you've tried or wished it away, it lingers long.

Empty.

Destitute. Vacant. Hollow. Meaningless. Hungry. Deprived of hope.

There seems to be no positive connotation to empty.

But . . .

There's another empty.

As we ponder another yearly celebration of Christ's resurrection, it's the empty I want to remember: the empty tomb of Jesus.

For what I received I passed on to you as of first importance: that Christ died for our sins according to the scriptures, that he was buried, that he was

*raised on the third day according to the Scriptures
. . . (1 Corinthians 15:3-4)*

For since death came through a man, the resurrection of the dead comes also through a man. For as in Adam all die, so in Christ all will be made alive. (1 Corinthians 15: 21-22)

This empty shouts of victory and not defeat! Freedom and not fear! Hope and not despair!

I want to linger long inside this empty . . . to always remember and never forget. It's not the empty that I've experienced before. It fills us up and gives us purpose, passion, and peace.

This is the empty that destroys my empty and infuses me with hope and new life. An empty that declares that my faith is by no means empty!

It is true that we don't ever come out of empty the way we went in; it changes us.

But can't we choose which empty impacts us the most?

I pray that the eyes of your heart may be enlightened in order that you may know the hope to which he has called you, the riches of his glorious inheri-tance in his holy people, and his incomparably great power for us who believe. That power is the same as the mighty strength he exerted when he raised Christ from the dead and seated him on his right hand in the heavenly realms. (Ephesians 1:18-20)

What about you?

How has emptiness impacted your life?
Are you damaged by the hollow emptiness felt
so often in this life?
Or are you restored by the powerful empty
we celebrate at Easter?
Why not take some time to consider just what the
empty tomb of Jesus really means to you?

Praise Focus: God is love,
and His mercy transforms my life.

Embracing the Grace of God in Life

*Out of the fullness of his **grace** he has blessed us all, giving us one blessing after another. (John 1:16)*

*Let us have confidence, then, and approach God's throne, where there is **grace**. There we will receive mercy and find **grace** to help us just when we need it. (Hebrews 4:16)*

Why Your Window is Important to Your Life

RECENTLY, I'VE BEEN INTRIGUED by windows. As I drive around the island, I seek them out.

Partly, because I'm looking for the survivors, the strong ones. The ones that fought the 185 mph winds of Hurricane Irma and won. But mostly, because I'm searching for the spark of hope that each new window represents. You see, our road to recovery following Hurricane Irma has been painfully slow, and any sign of rebuilding stands out like a beacon.

Focusing on these new windows is one little way I've chosen to see the beauty amid the brokenness. It doesn't matter that they're not my windows or that my home is still a long way away from being livable again. Just the sign of a new window going in fills me with hope. "Yay!" I say as I do a little victory dance in my head, "We're getting there, we're coming along!"

Then I ask, "Why did the homeowner choose this type of window?"

I see the louvers allowing for excellent ventilation, and the single hung ones allowing for maximum view, and I wonder about the trade-offs and the homeowners' decision-making process. How did they balance the need for fresh air and the desire for a beautiful view with the now pressing need for security and protection? How did they choose which was the right window for them?

It makes me think about the windows through which we choose to view our lives.

As a Christian, my window to the world is largely influenced by my faith in God. I've given over ownership to Him, and He gets to make the decisions. But, I'm still responsible for walking in obedience to Him.

For several years, I've had Philippians 4:8 plastered on my wall like a little window as a constant reminder of the peace that God offers if I choose to look through it: *Finally, brothers and sisters, whatever is true, whatever is noble, whatever is right, whatever is pure, whatever is lovely, whatever is admirable—if anything is excellent or praiseworthy—think about such things.*

Yet, many times, I choose not to sit at that window. Rather, I grumble and complain and nitpick. To be honest it's stifling. I don't have a good view of the world and am left open to attacks on my peace and contentment.

But recently, God has been calling me to come back to the window and sit with a view of life through Philippians 4:8. He asks me to trust that as Homeowner, He has made the best decision.

As windows are holding more and more of my interest, I'm beginning to fully appreciate the importance of choosing the window to my life.

Let me offer you two simple examples:

Windowpane 1

About a month ago, I came down with the flu. I hadn't had the flu in a long time, and this one was bad. I felt horrible. What's even worse, my daughter had it too. We were miserable and couldn't help each other.

Each day I would pray and hope that tomorrow I would feel better but, for well over a week, each new day brought a different flavor of bad.

One day, as we sat by the window feeling rather sorry for ourselves, I suggested to my daughter that perhaps we could paint a picture to brighten up our mood a bit.

"What should we paint?" she asked.

I replied, "What we see through the window." I looked up and focused on what I saw through the window—the broken branches and scars of a hurricane-bashed island looming larger than life. Given my state of mind, it seemed like a hopeless venture.

But then, I remembered my little Philippians 4:8 window. The one I'm choosing to view my life through.

"Well," I said, seeing the look of discouragement on her face, "we can focus on the bright blue of the sky, the sparkling blue sea and the green of the hills. Let's just focus on the good parts. There's beauty there."

Peace.

Windowpane 2

I wear a sparkly window around my neck. Well, it's not really a window; but it represents the window I'm choosing to sit next to during this season of my life.

It was a gift. A gift I didn't really want. A gift I thought was too extravagant. In fact, I had to bite my tongue from saying what I really wanted to say when my husband presented it to me.

I soon realized that rather than focusing on the expense of the gift, I could focus on my sweet husband's desire to bless his wife. I could Philippians 4:8 it.

Contentment.

It's just as the Homeowner promised. The window works remarkably well. In great matters or small, my God is still in control, and I can rest in Him.

So, I choose to keep wearing my new shiny pendant as a reminder. No matter what is happening on the outside, life is fresher, the view is better, and I'm protected from a horde of negative emotions and interactions when I keep Philippians 4:8 as my window.

What about you?

How is your window affecting your life?
Is your attention drawn to the brokenness
or the beauty that surrounds you?
Are you focusing on what you have or
on what you don't have?
Is your window framed with gratitude or entitlement?
Which window have you chosen to sit next to today?

Praise Focus: God is sovereign;
His commands are good for us.

Shattered Mirrors and My Messed Up Mercy

WHEN IT COMES TO mercy, I wish I could be more like a river, but sometimes I'm just a trickle.

Perhaps, it has something to do with the broken trinkets I lug around.

Like my magnifying glass. It works incredibly well, except it's broken. The focus is all off.

Huh? That doesn't make sense to you? Well, allow me to explain.

In moments when I encounter the folly of another wandering soul, another sojourner on this journey of life, I whip out my magnifier. With preposterous focus, it highlights the flaws and faults of the un-suspecting culprit until all else fades away.

Yet, when I turn this same lens back on me it has, not surprisingly, the opposite effect. With 20/20 vision, it shines the spotlight on my rightness, while any error on my part vanishes out of view.

Any logical person can sense that something is awry with my trusted magnifier, but I stubbornly hold on to it. Why wouldn't I? It strokes my ego just so.

A broken magnifier would be bad enough, but what's even worse is the shattered mirror I tote around. If it weren't so splintered, I could see the truth about myself. A clearer, more accurate reflection would be achieved. You know, the kind which shows that of all the sinners, I am chief. But no, so broken is it, that I don't see myself at all. What's even worst? It's been so long since it's reflected any-thing at all, that it's as though I've forgotten what I look like, forgotten the scars I try to hide.

Here is a trustworthy saying that deserves full ac-ceptance: Christ Jesus came into the world to save sinners—of whom I am the worst. (1 Timothy 1:15)

Anyone who listens to the word but does not do what it says is like someone who looks at his face in a mirror and, after looking at himself, goes away and immediately forgets what he looks like. (James 1:23-24)

This combination—magnifying the faults of others while not being able to get a good look at my-self—leads to the biggest problem of all. The broken shards of my mirror have poked holes in my fabric and allowed my empathy to leak right out of the bag. That inclusive sentiment—the one that comes alongside my brother, my friend—and whispers, "I understand. I walk the same road." The one that softens, welcomes, and loves with open arms. IT'S GONE! Slipped through the hole and right out of my heart without me even realizing it.

I think of the prodigal son and how much he had screwed up; how much he didn't deserve the reception he got. With my "if you know better, do better" justice scale, I am the older brother. I do not welcome this brother of mine. My scale, yet another gadget that stifles my mercy, vacillates between mercy and judgement, and settles on the side of judgement.

But judgement is heavy and the ache of dishing it out and living under it finally convicted me and made me realize that something was wrong. Something needed fixing, and I needed help.

Like the older brother, I, too, was in desperate need. I, too, needed mercy. With my goody-two-shoes-checklist personality, perhaps it took me longer to realize it.

So, I started first with the magnifier. Since the focus was totally off, and it was never intended to be used this way, I took it right back to the Manufacturer—my Father in Heaven. Thankfully, it was still under warranty. Yay for lifetime protection!

When I got it back, the difference was astonishing! Now all I could see were *specks* in my brother's eye while large *planks* and logs were floating around in my eyes. *(Matthew 7:3-5)* And that wasn't all. As much as I tried to keep it locked in his direction, it kept pulling and steering away from him, even from me, and pointing up toward God like a compass had been installed. It just kept refocusing on the amazing attributes of God and all that He has done for me. I didn't even remember it was supposed to work this way. It's like it was shouting to me, reminding me, "It's not about you, or him, or her. It's all about God."

My new mirror is even more amazing. It doesn't show the reflection I expected; the one that the world tells me is there; the one I believe I would have seen before. Rather, it's like seeing double. For each time I peer into this mirror, I see not just me but also my fellow believer. I see us as we really are—chosen and cherished children of God. I see the gold leaf of Jesus's blood that beautifully paints over our cracks and flaws . . . the scars we don't have to cover up when our story merges with God's beautiful story of redemption and opens our hearts to receive and give mercy.

And just like that, I see the shocking, ridiculous truth that God continually offers me mercy. Me, the older brother who doesn't show mercy very well.

But for that very reason I was shown mercy so that in me, the worst of sinners, Christ Jesus might display his immense patience as an example for those who would believe in him and receive eternal life. (1 Timothy 1:16)

Sometimes though, I find it hard to receive. I mean, when you stop to think about it, I really don't deserve it. I have this scale, you know, and it tips towards judgement even for, especially for, me.

But wincing under judgement is not a pleasant place to stay, and God calls to remind me that I'm fully known, yet loved, by Him. So I reach out and I feel it, too. The beautiful shock of a welcome party I really don't deserve.

I feel mercy.

I become the younger brother, fully aware of my transgressions and overjoyed by the sweet taste of mercy.

That helps me understand that my dear brother, sister, husband, friend, and I are in this together. We walk this path together. We all make missteps, sometimes intentionally, and we all need mercy. It's a moment pregnant with compassion, and my justice scale tips to the side of mercy.

Then it dawns on me—maybe I don't need to carry a scale at all. Maybe that's not my calling.

The trickle of mercy widens, and I am enabled to be merciful just as my Father is merciful. And *it is beautiful.*

What about you?

*Do you find it hard to receive the mercy God,
our Father, offers?
Are you towing around broken gadgets and scales that
mess up your ability to offer mercy to others?
Or are you a free-flowing river of God's mercy?*

*Praise Focus: God is merciful;
His mercies never come to an end;
they are new every morning.
(Lamentations 3:22-23 ESV)*

Looking for Thanks in All the Wrong Places

*And whatever you do, whether in word or deed, do
it all in the name of the Lord Jesus, giving thanks
to God the Father through him. (Colossians 3:17)*

I GLANCED UP AT the clock as a sliver of light fell
across the table. It was dawn, almost time to get
ready for the busy day ahead of me, and I had been
up most of the night. I could feel the strain in my
back, neck, and shoulders. I needed to get up and
stretch, to get moving. But I knew how important

it was to finish this project, so I kept going. Almost done, I told myself. Love lightens the load.

Later, as I sat wearily on my bed, stealing a few minutes before the craziness of another day crashed in on me, not only did my body ache, but my spirit did too.

I felt low. Unappreciated.

Have you ever felt that way? You worked hard, gave sacrificially of your time and effort, and even though you didn't do it for the thanks, your spirit sank just a little when no one seemed to notice.

I sat there thinking, "I wonder if he knows, if he understands the sacrifice it was." Yes, he had hurriedly mouthed thanks, but his obligatory word did little to convince me that he really appreciated my help. Sullenly, I mused, "Why can't he be more thankful?"

Isn't it funny how we accuse others of the very sins we are guilty of? There I was accusing my gracious and kind husband, while I was the one guilty of thanklessness.

That's when it started. From somewhere deep inside me . . . a slight flutter, unrecognizable at first. The stirring grew until a barely audible whisper escaped my mouth, "Thank you, Lord! Thank you for the opportunity to be of help to my husband. I am so blessed to be able to serve him in this way."

The cure was instantaneous. It was as if I had swallowed a magic pill. Gone was the sullen, discontented spirit; in its place was an overwhelming feeling of gratitude and peace.

As I went about my day with a new spring in my step, I chuckled about how I had stumbled upon the cure. Always there, right within my grasp, mine for the choosing—the cure for a disgruntled and sullen spirit. The choice to give thanks.

As I hummed the chorus of that old song by Johnny Lee, *Looking for Love in All the Wrong Places*,[12] aptly replacing love with "thanks" in the recesses of my mind, I smiled at the subtle ways God does some of His most amazing work in my life.

Rejoice always, pray continually, give thanks in all circumstances; for this is God's will for you in Christ Jesus. (1 Thessalonians 5:16-18)

As a glass half full kind of person, when it comes to the bigger issues of life, I customarily choose to focus on something to be thankful for, rather than ruminating on all that's wrong.

But often, in the nitty-gritty of every day, I forget to put on my thankful lens. Sometimes, I end up grumbling and complaining about the very things I ought to be thankful for. Ever happen to you? How absurd, right?

Just like that, I slip and slide right out of God's will for my life.

I don't know about you, but that is not a place I want to be. I want to be right up there under God's wings, abiding in His presence, *struggling with all His energy that He powerfully works within me (Colossians 1: 29 ESV)*.

The fact that this is even possible—that the Creator of heaven and earth has chosen me and *rides across the heavens to help (Deuteronomy 33:26)* me accomplish the good works He has prepared in advance for me to do—bowls me over and floods my spirit with thankfulness.

And when I choose to **live thankfully**, I am **blessed**. Happy. Blissful. With deep, internal happiness regardless of what is happening externally. A happiness that is not reliant on temporal things, like the praise of others or an anticipated thanks that feeds my flesh, but one that is wholly dependent on my relationship with God, my Father.

Yes, when I choose to remember the privileges I have in Him, and how grateful I am to be working in His kingdom, my life overflows with thanksgiving. And a disgruntled or discontented spirit has no chance to take root.

Moment by moment, I get to choose. Thankful or fretful? I get to choose to remain in the center of God's will for my life and, in doing so, open the floodgates for God's blessings to pour down.

How's that for a cure for a sulky spirit?

What about you?

*Have you fallen into the trap? Are you looking for thanks
in all the wrong places, or are you eagerly cultivating a
harvest of thanksgiving in your own life?
Remember, the choice is yours.
What do you choose to be thankful for right now?
Why don't you take a moment and list them all out?*

*Praise Focus: God is good and
gives us many reasons to thank Him.*

Why Love Demands That I Put Down My Chisel

IT'S DIFFICULT. THIS THING called love. It pulls me out of myself. Stretching me in ways that feel uncomfortable. Coaxing me to get up and help when I'd rather sit still. Then chiding me to be still when I'd rather scream and shout. It refuses to let me stay as I am while calling me to be the best "me" only I can be.

But most of all, it demands that I put down my chisel.

That's the hardest part. The part that I struggle with most. All along I thought that whipping out my chisel was just tough love. I mean, I could see it so clearly.

I have this knack, you know. I can see the chink in my loved ones' armor and, more times than not, I know a way to fix it. So out of sheer love (or so I tell myself), I reach for my handy chisel. I scrape and cut and pound and scrape, trying my best to smooth out the glaring flaw. Trying to make them shine the way I imagine they could.

Except, they resist. "Why can't they see what I'm seeing?" I think to myself. "This is for their good. If only they would comply, they'll understand too."

But when my chisel is in my hand with all of its subtle, yet unpleasant taps, controlling what my loved ones say, do, or even think, they don't feel loved.

Rather they feel judged, condemned, less than, and quite the opposite of what I intended.

And I've been there, too. I've felt judged and misunderstood rather than fully loved. I really don't want anyone I love to feel that way.

So, why do I keep returning to my chisel? Keep trying to fit my loved ones into the perfect mold I've envisioned for them?

Love has been calling to me for years . . . He whispers to me; He says to me, "Beloved, it's not your job. You're not called to fix; you're called to love. It's time to put down the chisel."

But I insist! Proudly walking around with my idea of love. Yet, I've caught glimpses of what it can be like when I place my chisel on the shelf. It feels right. My loved ones feel it, too.

Love is patient, love is kind.
It does not envy, it does not boast, it is not proud.
It does not dishonor others, it is not self-seeking,
it is not easily angered, it keeps no record of wrongs.
Love does not delight in evil but rejoices with the truth.
It always protects, always trusts, always hopes, always perseveres.
Love never fails.
(1 Corinthians 13:4-8a)

This weekend as my husband and I celebrated our 26th wedding anniversary, it dawned on me that our best times have coincided with those times when we have laid down our idea of love, with all of its tangled strings of pride and fear.

Once again, I'm reminded that loving the way God intends blossoms intimacy, peace, and growth.

In fact, our love—the way my husband loves me—gives me a sweet taste of God's rich love for us. It's a blessing I don't take for granted.

One would think that by now I would have it all figured out; that I would choose to remain in this circle of blessing. But no, I'm still tempted to pick up my chisel and fix him—perfect him.

But God keeps whispering, "Just as you are loved, you also ought to love." And that, my friend, is where it begins.

The realization of God's perfect love, graciously bestowed upon me by God Himself. A love that says I'm fully known, yet fully loved. A love that empowers me, by God's grace, to love others well.

Without God, I would remain powerless to love like this.

But God . . .

He continually pours into me His love, so rich and full, so undeserving, so freeing and empowering. It enables me to put my chisel down and truly share this thing called love.

What about you?

Do you remember to put your chisel down?
Do you freely offer the unconditional love of God?

Praise Focus: God is love, we can praise
Him because He loved us first.

What If God Listens the Way I Do?

I AM A GOOD listener.

At least, that's what my pride told me.

I believed it for a long time.

Even when it was clearly no longer true.

To be fair, I used to be a good listener.

I had learned the sacrifice well, honed it as a skill, and enjoyed the rewards.

But then, I got lazy.

I got selfish.

Well, to be honest, I am always selfish, but I allowed my selfishness to take over.

My *me*-ness rose to the surface, refused to be kept down, demanded its time.

And I stopped listening well.

It started off slowly.

Not giving my full attention while listening to my family . . .

Not taking the time to listen to those within my circle—those in need of sacrificial listening.

But then, the disease spread to my walk with God.

I would read His word and quickly forget the truths found within.

You could tell it in the way I lived: not convinced.

Not fully accepting who He says He is, what His intentions are, who He says I am, and how He longs for me to respond.

Instead of being quick to listen, I was often painfully slow.

Even worse, I loitered around instead of acting on His word.

What if God listens the way I do?

What if He becomes too distracted with all the thoughts in His mind to pay full attention to me, to us?

What if His sovereignty over His creations—this world, this universe—keeps Him so busy that He has no or very little time for me?

What if I was dying for Him to hear me, but He was unwilling to sacrifice the time, the attention, the love that listening requires?

What if?

But then the thought crashes in.

Who am I that God should listen to me?

Do I, a mere mortal made from a handful of dirt, dare open my mouth again to my Master? (Genesis 18:27b MSG)

I am reminded of my frailty, my unworthiness, my *filthy rags,* (Isaiah 64:6) and I wonder . . .

How can it be?

How can I in all of my sin and shame even consider the thought of approaching the Lord of this entire earth—the Lord enthroned in all-surpassing holiness—expecting Him to listen to me?

Yet, I am assured that He does listen:

The LORD is near to all who call on him, to all who call on Him in truth. (Psalm 145:18)

Then you will call on me and come and pray to me, and I will listen to you. You will seek me and find me when you seek me with all your heart. (Jeremiah 29:12-13)

I don't even have to speak the words for Him to hear.

Have you ever been there? Carrying a burden so large, desperately wanting to talk, but not being able to find the words? God listens even then.

Before a word is on my tongue you, LORD, know it completely. (Psalm 139:4)

And my unworthiness, my unrighteousness doesn't even block the way, for I am assured that as a child of God, Christ's righteousness flings open the doors for me.

Therefore, since we have been justified through faith, we have peace with God through our Lord Jesus Christ, through whom we have gained access by faith into this grace in which we now stand. (Romans 5:1-2a)

Let us then approach God's throne of grace with confidence, so that we may receive mercy and find grace to help us in our time of need. (Hebrews 4:16)

Did you get that?
Access to God.
Approach with confidence.
Receive mercy.
Find grace.
When I ponder these precious truths, they pierce my soul, bring me to my knees, and infuse me with a renewed desire.
A desire to be still.

Stand still, and consider the wondrous works of God. (Job 37:14b KJV)

A desire to be slow to speak.

Be still, and know that I am God; I will be exalted among the nations, I will be exalted in the earth. (Psalm 46:10)

A desire to listen.

Make me to know your ways, O Lord; teach me your paths. Lead me in your truth and teach me; for you are the God of my salvation; for you I wait all the day long. (Psalm 25:4-5 ESV)

To listen wholeheartedly to the One who, incredibly, listens to my heart, my thoughts, my words. I want to savor my time with Him.

And when I listen, I hear His heart.

I hear . . .

. . . His desire for me to sacrifice my time, my attention, my love, my prideful hunger to be heard.

. . . His desire for me to reflect His listening heart to those He places in my path.

. . . His desire for me to be a good listener.

What about you?

*When did you last consider the amazing truth
that God listens to you?
Does this truth motivate you to be a better listener?
Which is your favorite listening scripture?*

*Praise Focus: God is merciful; He cares for
us and welcomes us into His presence.*

Focus on the Passengers, Not on the Road

I DON'T KNOW WHEN my obsession with driving from the passenger seat started. I want to say that it was one of my husband's infamous wrong turns that started it. Maybe instead of staying right, we turned left. Maybe the time lost and resulting inconvenience piqued my interest and heightened my senses. But that wouldn't be honest. For no matter how many times we've made a wrong turn, we've always found our way again. Besides, my husband seldom makes wrong turns.

Wrong turns may be a bit unsettling, but usually they are no big deal.

Usually.

That's just the thing. When you're in unfamiliar surroundings and you make a wrong turn, you're never quite sure where you'll end up. Right there at that moment, you have no way of knowing just how bothersome or even dangerous this turn off might be.

The not knowing—that's the part I don't like. You see, I like to be in the know. I like to know where I'm going and how I'm getting there.

So, this summer, as we vacationed in Orlando, I might not have been the driver, but my eyes were on the road. Just in case, you know, just in case the driver (my-great-with-directions-husband) failed to pay attention and made a wrong turn.

It's like I somehow felt that my involvement, my focus on the road, and my well-timed nudges would prevent any unnecessary or unexpected detours.

But God has a way of teaching us big truths in the little moments of life, and he had one in store for me this summer.

You see, despite my watchful, controlling gaze, my husband did make a wrong turn. And you know what? It was a bit inconvenient and caused us to arrive later than we had anticipated, but it was all right; no big deal.

Furthermore, he drove several times without the security that my presence assures (who am I kidding?) and he was quite fine. He actually got where he was going in one piece.

Then that it dawned on me: Maybe I can just relax. Take my eyes off the road. But let me tell you, it was work! It's not easy for a control-girl to release the reins. But I tried.

As I relaxed, I realized something.

Instead of multitasking, splitting my attention here, there, and everywhere (mainly on the road), I was able to focus solely on my daughter. We joked, laughed, and enjoyed the passing sites. We had a refreshing conversation.

It truly was a delight.

It got me to thinking about my spiritual life.

As a Christian, I've long since handed the wheel over to God, but that doesn't mean that I don't still try to drive from the passenger seat.

I keep my eyes fixed on the road because, you know, I know where I want to go and I know how I want to get there.

I try to let God know, as often as I can, that I don't like wrong turns. Don't like the inconvenience and the time or pain that it takes to get back on track. Back on the path that I think I should be on.

But Jesus keeps whispering to me, "I know where I'm taking you, and I Am the Way to get there. Trust me. *Don't* let the destination distract you from the heart of the matter. Focus on the passengers. Be my hands and feet."

That advice is playing over and over in my mind as we get ready to start our sixth year homeschooling. A journey that hasn't necessarily followed the path I had in mind; I tend to focus on the road, on the destination I have planned. But God is whispering, "Focus on the passengers and let Me do the driving."

It's the hope-filled wisdom I will need in the nitty-gritty of the daily grind. When my eyes are fixed on the road and the wrong turns come; when life doesn't unfold as I imagine it should; I will need to remember Who's driving and focus on the passengers.

I will need to remember my role as God's ambassador, showing Him to a hurting people—fellow travelers along the way. I will need to see interruptions as opportunities to minister for Him.

I will need to simply love them like Jesus.

And wrong turns? They are not actually wrong. They are filled with purpose and designed by God to draw me closer to Him and make me more like Him.

My head knows this, but my heart says, "It's scary not knowing when a wrong turn may occur or which road it will take me down." But God's plans for me and my children are perfect. His presence will never leave me.

So, I can trust Him because, ultimately, I know what He wants for me and it is good.

Jesus answered, "I am the way and the truth and the life. No one comes to the Father except through me." (John 14:6)

Now this is eternal life: that they may know you, the only true God, and Jesus Christ, whom you have sent. (John 17:3)

Therefore be imitators of God, as beloved children. And walk in love, as Christ loved us and gave

Himself up for us, a fragrant offering and sacrifice to God. (Ephesians 5: 1-2 ESV)

• 179 •

"A new command I give you: Love one another. As I have loved you, so you must love one another." (John 13:34)

What about you?

*Are you a passenger driver or have you
handed over full control?
What road are you so focused on that
you forget the passengers?
Are you missing opportunities to love them like Jesus?
Why not take a moment to reflect today and
trust God to do the driving?*

*Praise Focus: God is sovereign;
He can be trusted for our salvation.*

How I Get Back Up When My Mirror Tears Me Down

HAVE YOU EVER WALKED past a store window and caught a glimpse of your reflection and gasped? In silent confusion, you wonder, "What? When did that happen?"

Ever had one of those moments? You realize that you don't look the way you imagined you did?

Well, it happened to me recently, and I'm still recovering from the shock.

No, it's not what you think. I wasn't startled by a physical mirror depicting an older, less fit me. Instead, it was the mirror of my peers.

Someone, not just anyone, but someone close to me used the word "irritable" to describe me. It was a quick, off-the-cuff remark, but I felt it like a punch to the gut. I took it like a big girl, but the ache lingered long.

Irritable? How come I didn't see that when I looked in the mirror?

Yes, I know that sometimes I'm a bit grouchy after nine at night, especially when sleep is pulling me under. Everyone close to me knows that—it's just how I am. My family accepts that . . . I think.

Or sometimes I can be a little impatient with negative or judgemental people. I mean, their infectious negativity floods my spirit and drains me.

"It's not my fault," I muse. "You would do the same thing if you were in my shoes. And besides, this short fuse runs in my family."

Do you hear it? The way I try to justify my irritability and explain away my bad behavior? The way that my pride has sneaked in and convinced me that this little sin is justifiable and acceptable!

It seems my battle with pride never goes away. Just when I think I have it mastered, it raises its ugly head. Here it was masquerading as a mirror, acting like a veil, but blocking the real mirror of my soul—the word of God.

As a Christian, I desire to reflect the love of God and let His light shine through me in this dark world. God instructs me in His word not to merely hear the word, but to do it. As a servant of Christ, that is my joy-filled obligation.

Yet, here I was being told that I really wasn't doing such a great job: my desire and my actions didn't match up well. I long to reflect Christ, but what others are actually seeing is me standing in the way.

It seems like I often take over and block Christ out of the way. Even worse, I feel completely justified in doing so.

"It's just the way I am," I lie to myself.

It's the age-old battle of flesh vs. spirit.

I hang my head in shame. Once again, I've let God down.

With my bruised pride, I wonder how to approach Him, yet again, with the same old failure.

I'm tired of this cycle, and I know now that I'm not strong enough to break it. So, God is teaching me how to love when He bruises my pride.

To be honest, I don't relish it at first; it's humiliating, embarrassing, and downright painful.

I feel like a failure, like I'm really bad at . . . well, in this case, I'm really bad at being really good for God.

Wait, hang on one minute, is that what it means to be a Christian? That I must be really good to please God?

It is then I breathe a sigh of relief. I exhale the lies before they consume me and inhale the grace of God.

Once again, He patiently guides me on a journey from bruised pride to the sweet harvest of a closer walk with Him.

It's not always an easy journey. Okay, it's never an easy journey, but it is so worth it. Over time, be it minutes or months, God gently leads me from bruised pride to humility, through complete confession and genuine repentance. He leads me to a fuller dependence on Him in my daily walk.

It starts with remembering that it's all about God, not me.

Not my ability, but God's. Not my light, but His.

It's all about Him and His grace.

Or do you think Scripture says without reason that he jealously longs for the spirit he has caused to dwell in us? But he gives us more grace. That is why Scripture says, "God opposes the proud, but shows favor to the humble." Humble yourselves before the Lord, and he will lift you up. (James 4:5-6, 10)

Once I accept my weakness, I open myself up to accept more grace.

Did you get that? He gives us more grace, but sometimes we refuse to receive it. Sometimes, in our pride, we attempt to live a victor's life by relying on our own ability rather than His grace. Then we beat ourselves up when we can't keep up. But I can't do it; I need help. So, I adjust my posture, bow low before Him, and admit my sin, humbly asking for and receiving His help.

Then I arm myself with the only weapon of offense proven to be successful in this battle—the sword of the Spirit—the Word of God.

When I'm tempted to follow my own selfish desires, be irritable or easily offended, justify my grumbling and complaining, or give in to the prideful me trying to enslave me . . .

When I'm cowering in the shadows, feeling ashamed that I've failed yet again, whichever temptation or lie of the enemy I'm facing . . .

I can fight back with the truth of God's Word.

And God is able to bless you abundantly, so that in all things at all times, having all that you need, you will abound in every good work. (2 Corinthians 9:8)

And that, my friends, is how I get back up when my mirror tears me down! It is the sword I'm choosing to fight with.

Yep, on my own, I fail to reflect Christ. But God has promised that He will complete the *good work* that He has started in me *(Philippians 1:6)*, and I'm taking Him at His word.

I may not be there yet, but there is hope. God reminds me that I'm saved by grace, empowered to do His will. I can get back up, receive the grace God continually gives me, and share it willingly as I reflect Him to a world of people just like me— people in desperate need of His saving grace.

What about you?

Which sins keep pulling you back down?
How are you choosing to battle them?
Take heart, my friend,
you can get back up
and fight.

Praise Focus: God is merciful;
He supplies all that we need to live for Him.

The Sweet Taste of Mercy When You Have Done Wrong

TEARS STREAMED DOWN HER face as she came to me. She had done wrong, and she knew it. Not just wrong . . . doubly wrong. The weight of her misdeeds crushed her spirit, and she sobbed.

How will she tell him what she has done? How will he ever trust her again?

Pleadingly, she looked at me. "Can you tell him?" she implored.

But I knew it could not be. I could not carry this burden for her. She must be the one to confess.

And so, between wails, she told her brother what she had done and she waited.

Waited in nervous apprehension of his judgement. She knew what she deserved, and it scared her. He would be angry. He would give her a most disapproving look that would send her cowering in shame. He would withdraw from her and withhold his friendship. She shuddered at the sheer thought of it as she waited.

I, too, waited. But as I waited, I prayed.

I prayed for the one who had done wrong, and I prayed for me . . . for wisdom to remain calm and gently point them to God. But mostly I prayed for the brother offended. For this is the brother who often needed to be reminded to temper justice with mercy . . . to tone down his interactions with others with a touch of compassion. So, I prayed for God to soften his heart.

Then came the judgement. He was angry, justifiably so. There was no outburst, just quiet, seething indignation. In his mind, he had been wronged, and he had the right to be upset. She would buy them back. It was as simple as that. She had broken what was his, and she should replace it.

But she was unable to do this because the cost was prohibitive. There was no way she could replace them. Even so, as we all do when we find ourselves in these unnerving predicaments, she tried to right her wrong.

"I'm really sorry!" she lamented as she offered her brother a list of services she would render. He could choose any three on the list, and she would willingly and happily oblige in a desperate attempt to fix what was broken. She would do this for the next several weeks. She knew she could not easily and on her own replace her brother's property, but she could try to restore the damaged relationship between them.

That simple, handwritten outpouring of her heart reminded me of me . . . of so many of us who try to repay.

We have done wrong.

Against you, you only, have I sinned and done what is evil in your sight; so you are right in your verdict and justified when you judge. (Psalm 51:4)

And we desperately try to right our wrongs.

Sometimes, we spend our whole lives trying to make right what we have done wrong. We willingly accept suffering and feelings of guilt and shame, as if somehow deep down, we believe that by paying one's dues we make up for past mistakes. We offer our best efforts hoping that they would, in some way, help to rectify our misdeeds.

"But they are still broken!" he insisted. He was stating the obvious—nothing she could say or do could undo what had been done. His precious possession was still damaged.

My son's curt response reminded me that there is nothing we can do to fix our sin problem. No way for us to right our wrong.

". . . all our righteous acts are like filthy rags; we all shrivel up like a leaf and like the wind our sins sweep us away." (Isaiah 64:6)

Once again, his stance was one of justice. But where was the mercy?

Prayerfully, I shared with him a story. A story of mercy shown to him. He had damaged something too, once. Something much more valuable, something he could not replace or pay for. And yet he had been forgiven of the offense, and it had not been held against him. I reminded him of God's mercy towards us and invited him to share that mercy with his sister.

He looked at her list and then nonchalantly laid it aside. "They are still broken," he said. But this time his tone was different, softer.

You do not delight in sacrifice, or I would bring it; you do not take pleasure in burnt offerings. My sacrifice, O God, is a broken spirit; a broken and contrite heart you, God, you will not despise. (Psalm 51:16-17)

Then quietly and subtly, he did it. He extended an olive branch. An offer of peace during a time of strife, a gift of reconciliation, a restoration of sweet fellowship.

The next day, the sounds of merriment and laughter filled our home. My daughter was giddy with happiness. She could not believe her good fortune. She had done wrong, had agonized through the pain of confession, had expected his justifiable wrath, but instead had been blessed with unexplained and unimaginable forgiveness and acceptance.

I sat there in utter gratitude, thankful for the sweet rapport I was witnessing and amazed at how my God continues to reach me and teach me in the everyday circumstances of my life.

You see, my God knew. He knew that I needed to be reminded to temper justice with mercy.

It's a constant daily struggle. I need to remember the mercy He has shown me, and I need to extend that same mercy to others.

Just like that, through a child's mistake, my God showed me, once again, what it was like to savor the sweet taste of mercy.

My God is holy and just and merciful. And oh so personal.

"Who am I? That the eyes that see my sin would look on me with love, and watch me rise again."[13]

"These are the ones I look on with favor: those who are humble and contrite in spirit; and who tremble at my word." (Isaiah 66:2b)

If we confess our sins, he is faithful and just and will forgive us our sins and purify us from all unrighteousness. (1 John 1:9)

"Whoever comes to me I will never drive away." (John 6:37b)

What about you?

Have you experienced the sweet taste of mercy?
Or are you exhausted, trying hard to right your wrongs?
Do you share that mercy with others?

Praise Focus: God is merciful;
He welcomes a repentant sinner
with joy and gladness.

Facing Your Tainted Reflection with Courage and Grace

"No, Mommy, you were angry!" her words still echo in my mind.

I remember it well. There I was retelling the incident to my children, hoping to use my example to instill in them the importance of having faith in God, when it happened.

I came face to face with my reflection, the me that my children see, and it wasn't pretty.

I sat stunned. The broken pride in me wanting to shout out, "No, that's not how it was!"

But as reality slowly sunk in, I realized that they were right and I was wrong. I hung my head in shame; my fantasy of how well I had portrayed my Heavenly Father shattered. The reality—my reflection was tainted. In that moment, and perhaps countless others that I'm probably not even aware of, my actions did not point to God. I failed to show them Jesus.

It took courage then, to apologize and say I was sorry for failing to model Christ-like behavior.

It took a kiss of grace, mercifully offered by my Father in heaven, to **keep calm and shine on.**

That phrase is stuck in my memory. It came to me during the year of my father's illness. I was feeling such pressure. Often away from home, whether physically or mentally, as I cared for my father, I worried about my children. How was I to do it all? How was I to facilitate their success this year in homeschool? I was so distracted, yet I kept sensing the Lord telling me to *keep calm and shine on.*

Despite all the pressure, the fear of failure, the raw emotions of loved ones, the feelings of inadequacy, the uncertainty of the future; simply **keep**

calm (it's as if He was telling me—remember who I Am) and **shine on** (live for me, serve me, simply do the next right thing . . . the one that brings me glory).

Here again, God was speaking to my heart. "Keep calm and shine on," He said. "Yes, you messed up, and yes, you continue to fall short of My glory, but remember who I Am. I am full of mercy and grace. Simply, shine on. Point them to Me. Let them see you turn to Me. Let them see the grace of forgiveness. Let them see that even an imperfect portrayal is not the end. There is hope, always hope."

But we have this treasure in jars of clay to show that this all-surpassing power is from God and not from us. We are hard pressed on every side, but not crushed; perplexed, but not in despair; persecuted, but not abandoned; struck down, but not destroyed. (2 Corinthians 4:7-9)

And so, I raised my head as I found the courage and grace that I needed. The power so lavishly supplied by my Father in heaven not only to apologize to my children, but to point them to our Heavenly Father—the only perfect One.

So, my friend, I understand the pressure to ensure your walk matches your talk. I also understand the pride which tells you that your actions, whether good or bad, have incredible power. Power to heal or to harm. That if you mess up, somehow you have damaged your fellowship with God—not to mention your reputation and His. But I also know grace. And God, so gently and persistently, reminds me that it is not my perfection that counts but His; not my perfection that gets me to my heavenly home or into a right relationship with Him, but His. I am saved by grace. I am so thankful for grace. Thankful that no matter how many times I mess up, grace is always there welcoming me back home.

What about you?

Are you tired of messing up repeatedly?
Do you need a fresh kiss of God's grace today?

Praise Focus: God is love and full of grace and mercy.

When My Life is Not Music to the Ears

He put a new song in my mouth, a hymn of praise to our God. Many will see and fear the LORD and put their trust in him. (Psalm 40:3 ESV)

I LAY IN MY hotel bed, pen in hand, trying to figure out what I would say.

Where were the words?

Words that would string together the years of prayers and tears, hopes and fears, and give him wings to fly. Words that would slip seamlessly underneath and bear him up when life pulls him down. Words that would echo in his ears, pulling him away from danger when temptations lurk near. Words that would encourage, inspire, warn, guide, but most importantly, love.

Where were the words?

In just a few short days, I would be returning home without my teenaged son. He would literally be on his own. For the first time in his life.

On. His. Own.

Oh, how I wanted to leave him with the right words. Words that would be a rock to stand on, a pillow to rest on, and a friend to hold close. As I stood on the brink of a never-before, I searched for these words.

What words would you have used? What would you have said?

When the words started to flow, they wouldn't stop. Dripping from my heart, they filled page after page; there was always something more to share.

But then I paused. This was not the time to waste words.

I reflected on what I had written . . . "I encourage you to always be thankful. Each day is filled with many good gifts; we just sometimes must look for them. Always give God thanks for something . . . everyday . . . even on the down days.

Please don't ever turn your back on God.

I'm thankful for Jesus who willingly took on the wrath that I deserved so now I don't have to. I can live freely—free from fear, and happy.

You can always come to me no matter what."

I looked at the words that had dripped through my fingers, and I wondered, "Was this all just noise?"

You see, as I lay there writing to my firstborn, I became acutely aware of the sound our lives make. As one who professes to follow Christ, is my life-song music to the ears or simply noise? Do I live my faith out loud? Or does it just look like empty words? Does my relationship with Christ impact all aspects of my life? My relationships? My goals? My reactions to life's challenges?

As Christians, when our actions mirror our words of faith, the beautiful authenticity displayed is almost melodic as it gently calls, "Come, come meet the One who knows all about me and loves me even so."

Music to the ears. Pleasing. An invitation to know the transforming power of a relationship with Christ.

But then there is the noise. The grating hypocrisy when sweet-sounding words are betrayed by off-key, rules-based, judgemental actions that cause others to put their hands to their ears and run for cover.

Irritating. Harsh. Noise.

I wondered what sound my son heard. From my words? And from my life?

I glanced again at my words on the pages. How would they be received? As grace-filled notes of a beautiful melody? Irresistibly compelling? Or wrought meaningless by the disharmony of my off-key actions?

I needed to be careful here. If I listened to the enemy, he would try to convince me that the imperfect harmony of my life plays loud and clear, stripping me of my witness.

But I knew the truth. I knew that there was another tune evident in my life. The ever-present, sweet sound of God's beautiful redemption music.

The tune that keeps beckoning me and doesn't stop singing of God's love for me, no matter how often I wander away. It empowers me to live for Him and to share His love through the song of my words and the dance of my actions.

It's a tune that I pray plays above all of the other sounds in my life. And one that I pray my son hears in my life and resonates in his heart as he reads my words.

> "But His favorite song of all
> *Is the song of the redeemed*
> When those purchased by His blood
> *Lift to Him a song of love.*"[14]

What about you?

What sound is playing loudest in your life?
The grating sound of self-righteous actions and attitudes?
Or the sweet harmony of a heart continually
bowed before God?

Praise Focus: God is love,
and His mercy knows no bounds.

What Does Living Look Like to You?

Lean in close.

I want to ask you something.

It's a bit personal.

I'm sorry. I usually don't do this. I understand you're a private person. I am, too. I would never do this ordinarily.

But this is too important.

How do I know?

Because I've seen it. Seen it in the eyes of the dying.

On the brink of death, there it was—the burning desire to live fully.

So, I'm asking you . . .

What does living look like to you?

No, don't answer. Not yet.

It's a question you need to chew on, to digest slowly, to mull over and over.

Some of us envision the doing life.

We are the ones who feel most alive when we are doing. Doing a lot. Doing big. Doing what brings happiness, wealth, success, or recognition. You get the point.

Then there are those of us who are nestled comfortably in the being camp. For us, it's more important to be true to who we are. We don't get too caught up in the doing, we're happy just to be. Or so we say.

But each camp looks longingly at the other and wonders . . .

Am I missing something?

And with all the doing, and being, and longing, sometimes we miss the simple, sweet story that's as old as time.

It's like a fairy tale.

It's full of wonder and transports us to a place where anything is possible.

It exists outside our time, yet within our time.

And it's filled with excitement and anticipation.

Yes, it's very much like a fairy tale, except that it's not.

Its truth whispers to our souls, and we just know.

We know that it's real.

And if we let it, it comforts and reassures us.

But we complicate things; we muddy the waters.

We don't believe that the living we seek could be so simple.

God willingly and graciously offers us LIFE and promises to reveal to us the way, but we hesitate. Not fully persuaded it's what we want.

So, we turn away.

It happened once upon a time, a long time ago in a garden.

And still, it happens once upon a time every day in our own time.

We miss the point, miss the sincerity, and miss the love behind the invitation.

We miss the simplicity and amazing possibility of life as it could be . . .

A close, sweet walk with the LORD—the Writer of the story . . .

An enduring, intimate relationship with the merciful, gracious, long-suffering God who is forever abundant in goodness and truth . . .

Fellowship with the God who lovingly weaves us into His story, knowing that only therein can we truly live.

You will make known to me the path of life; In Your presence is fullness of joy; In Your right hand there are pleasures forever. (Psalm 16:11 ESV)

You see, my question— "What does living look like to you?"—has many layers.

What I'm really asking is . . .

Deep down in your heart, do you really trust the heart of God?

Do you truly believe that in His presence you will find what living really looks like?

Are you fully convinced that He has, in fact, given us everything we need for life?

Are you building on the starter pack He has given you?

So don't lose a minute in building on what you've been given, complementing your basic faith with good character, spiritual understanding, alert discipline, passionate patience, reverent wonder, warm friendliness, and generous love, each dimension fitting into and developing the others. With these qualities active and growing in your lives, no grass will grow under your feet, no day will pass without its reward as you mature in your experience of our Master Jesus. (2 Peter 1:5-8 MSG)

Or do you feel that you are better suited to manage your own affairs? To design life as you wish?

I told you it was personal.

But I'll share something with you.

Several years ago, when I peered into the eyes of the dying, when I saw there the intense yearning for living, I vowed that I would live each gift-day to the fullest.

Despite my vow, I kept feeling like I was missing something and that I wasn't living fully.

As I sought the Lord, I felt God calling me to live amazed.

To live amazed by who He is, what He has done, and what He is doing.

As I gaze into His word and His world, savoring the beauty, the goodness, the love, the mercy, the power of the LORD, I am finding that living amazed looks a lot like clinging to Him, listening to Him, and accepting His power to live for Him.

I am humbled that the all-powerful God invites me to cling to Him, weaves me into His timeless love story, and empowers me to cultivate a life that brings Him glory.

I'm praying that every day I'll remember this life-changing truth and live amazed.

So, I'll ask you again, what does living look like to you?

A Personalized Promise for You From God's Heart to Yours

When you need to remember what God has given you, or you need encouragement to claim His great and precious promises so that you can Live Amazed!

God's divine power has given me everything I need for life and for godliness. This power was given to me through knowledge of the One who called me by His own glory and integrity. Through His glory and integrity He has given me His promises that are of the highest value. Through these promises I will share in the divine nature because I have escaped the corruption that sinful desires cause in the world.
(2 Peter 1:3-4, author's paraphrase)

Stay Amazed - Verses for Meditation

May my meditation be pleasing to him, for I rejoice in the LORD. (Psalm 104:34)

God invites us to know Him and reveals Himself through His Word and world. Every day is a new opportunity to discover more about Him and to live amazed at who He is. Below you'll find a list of some of God's attributes along with selected corresponding verses. Take time to ponder the greatness of our God by choosing to meditate on these verses. You can write them out, use them in your prayers, or commit them to memory, the choice is yours. Simply come to God expectantly and allow Him to wow you with His presence.

Eternality (God is everlasting)	Patience (God is long-suffering)
Psalm 90:1-2	Nehemiah 9:17
Psalm 102:12	Joel 2:13
Isaiah 40:28	Psalm 86:15
Colossians 1:15-17	Romans 2:4
Revelation 1:8	2 Peter 3:9
Foreknowledge (God knows the future)	**Love (God is loving)**
Job 14:5	Isaiah 49:15-16
Psalm 139:16	Hosea 11:4
Isaiah 46:9-10	Romans 5:8
Matthew 6:8	Titus 3:4-7
1 Peter 1:20	1 John 4:8-10
Goodness (God is good)	**Mercy (God is merciful)**
Nahum 1:7	Deuteronomy 4:31
Psalm 25:8	Psalm 116:5
Psalm 145:8-9	Micah 7:18-19
Matthew 5:45	Luke 1:78-79
Acts 14:17	1 Peter 1:3

Immutability (God never changes)	**Omnipotence (God is all powerful)**
Malachi 3:6	Genesis 1:1-3
Psalm 102:25-27	Psalm 33:6-9
Romans 11:29	Daniel 4:17
Hebrews 13:8	Hebrews 1:3
James 1:17	Revelation 19:6
Incomprehensibility (God is unfathomable)	**Omnipresence (God is always everywhere)**
Job 11:7-9	Deuteronomy 31:6
Ecclesiastes 3:11	Psalm 139:7-12
Isaiah 40:12-31	Isaiah 43:2
Isaiah 55:8-9	Jeremiah 23:23-24
1 Corinthians 2:16	Matthew 28:20
Infinity (God is without limits)	**Sovereignty (God is in control)**
1 Kings 8: 27	Psalm 135:6-7
Psalm 100:5	Daniel 4:35
Psalm 147:5	John 1:1-3
Isaiah 66:1-2	Romans 9:20
Romans 11:33	Revelation 4:11

The Amazing Gospel Story

We all have a story.
Each uniquely ours.
But we are also part of a much bigger story,
an amazing story, God's story.

Who is God?
The creator of the universe:

You alone are the LORD. You made the heavens, even the highest heavens, and all their starry host, the earth and all that is on it, the seas and all that is in them. You give life to everything, and the multitudes of heaven worship you. (Nehemiah 9:6)

What is He like?
In His own words:

Then the LORD passed by in front of him and proclaimed, "The LORD, the LORD God, compassionate and gracious, slow to anger, and abounding in lovingkindness and truth; who keeps lovingkindness for thousands, who forgives iniquity, transgression and sin; yet He will by no means leave the guilty unpunished. (Exodus 34:6-7 NASB)

Can we know Him?

We may not fully understand Him, but we can know Him:

You will seek me and find me when you seek me with all your heart. (Jeremiah 29:13)

And we know that the Son of God has come, and he has given us understanding so that we can know the true God. (1 John 5:20a NLT)

Why are we here?

God created us in His image, to be His children, and to bring Him glory. It's all part of His plan:

For we are the temple of the living God. As God has said: "I will live with them and walk among them, and I will be their God, and they will be my people. (2 Corinthians 6:16a)

But something is not right. What went wrong?
We rebelled:

Choosing to satisfy self and rebel against God led to separation and disharmony. This disharmony exists within each one of us, between God and us, among people, and between people and the earth.

For all have sinned and fall short of the glory of God. (Romans 3:23)

Indeed, there is no one on earth who is righteous, no one who does what is right and never sins. (Ecclesiastes 7:20)

How does God respond?
God must be true to His character. He is holy:

He will by no means leave the guilty unpunished. (Exodus 34:7b NASB)

For it is written, "Be holy, because I am holy." (1 Peter 1:16)

For the wages of sin is death. (Romans 6:23a)

Yet God is also merciful. By His great mercy, knowing that we can by no means save ourselves, God provided a means of escape from the punishment we all deserve:

For while we were still helpless, at the right time Christ died for the ungodly. For one will hardly die for a righteous man; though perhaps for the good man someone would dare even to die. But God demonstrates His own love toward us, in that while we were yet sinners, Christ died for us. (Romans 5: 6-8 NASB)

For the wages of sin is death, but the gift of God is eternal life in Christ Jesus our Lord. (Romans 6:23)

What can I do?
Turn away from your sins and believe God:

"The time has come," he said. "The kingdom of God has come near. Repent and believe the good news!" (Mark 1:15)

They replied, "Believe in the Lord Jesus, and you will be saved." (Acts 16:31)

'If you declare with your mouth, "Jesus is Lord," and believe in your heart that God raised him from the dead, you will be saved. For it is with your heart that you believe and are justified, and it is with your mouth that you profess your faith and are saved.' (Romans 10: 9-10)

'We implore you on Christ's behalf: Be reconciled to God. God made him who had no sin to be sin for us, so that in him we might become the righteousness of God.' (2 Corinthians 5: 20b-21)

'Very truly I tell you, whoever hears my word and believes him who sent me has eternal life and will not be judged but has crossed over from death to life.' (John 5: 24)

You can live amazed!

The thief comes only to steal and kill and destroy; I have come that they may have life, and have it to the full. (John 10:10)

Index – Topics
(chapter #)

Index –
Devotions

About the Author

CARLA LAKE HAS FOUND many reasons to live amazed. As a wife of 27 years to one wonderfully kind and generous man, mom to two teenaged blessings, and a daughter, sister, friend to an incredibly loyal and supportive gang, she often finds herself in awe of God who pours blessings into her life.

Through her passion for writing about God's promises, Carla hopes to spread the aroma of the knowledge of Christ from her little corner of the Caribbean.

A lover of nature, Carla is often found in jeans and a t-shirt, savoring the simpler things and finding life lessons in unexpected places. She is slightly obsessed with wildflowers, chocolate, and the color green.

You can connect with her on her blog: 'From Dust Towards the Heavens' at www.lcasvi.blogspot.com or follow her on:

Facebook: www.Facebook.com/
fromdusttowardstheheavens

Twitter: @Carlielakevi

Instagram: @from.dust.towards.the.heavens

Endnotes

1   Union and Communion with God the End and Design of the Gospel. Accessed May 09, 2019. https://biblehub.com/sermons/auth/binning/union_and_communion_with_god_the_end_and_design_of_the_gospel.htm.

2   Tozer, A. W. *The Knowledge of the Holy: The Attributes of God: Their Meaning in the Christian Life*. San Francisco, Ca.: Harper San Francisco, 1992.

3   Bible Presbyterian Church Online: WSC Question 4. Accessed March 09, 2016. http://www.shortercatechism.com/resources/wsc/wsc_004.html.

4   Spurgeon, Charles Haddon. "The Immutability of God." Spurgeon. January 07, 1855. Accessed March 09, 2016. https://www.spurgeon.org/resource-library/sermons/the-immutability-of-god#flipbook/.

5   Spurgeon, Charles Haddon. "The Immutability of God." Spurgeon. January 07, 1855. Accessed March 09, 2016. https://www.spurgeon.org/resource-library/sermons/the-immutability-of-god#flipbook/.

6   "Your Joy Rests on Jesus's Righteousness." Desiring God. May 09, 2019. Accessed February 16, 2017. https://www.desiringgod.org/articles/your-joy-rests-on-jesuss-righteousness.

7   Ulrich, Philip, and Erin Ulrich. *Morning*. Lexington, Kentucky: Here We Go Productions, 2014.

8   Carroll, Amy. *Breaking up with Perfect: Kiss Perfection Good-bye and Embrace the Joy God Has in Store for You*. Nashville: Howard Books, 2015.

9   "Tenth Avenue North – I Have This Hope." Genius. September 10, 2016. Accessed November 06, 2017. https://genius.com/Tenth-avenue-north-i-have-this-hope-lyrics.

10 Michelle, Erika. "Open My Eyes November Scripture Writing Plan." A Symphony of Praise. October 28, 2016. Accessed November 02, 2016. https://asymphonyofpraise.com/blog/open-my-eyes-november-scripture-writing.

11 "Experience the Bible Daily with the YouVersion." YouVersion. Accessed February 05, 2017. https://www.youversion.com/.

12 "Johnny Lee – Lookin' For Love." Genius. August 01, 1980. Accessed September 23, 2016. https://genius.com/Johnny-lee-lookin-for-love-lyrics.

13 "Casting Crowns – Who Am I." Genius. October 07, 2003. Accessed August 13, 2017. https://genius.com/Casting-crowns-who-am-i-lyrics.

14 "Phillips, Craig & Dean – Favorite Song of All." Genius. Accessed March 24, 2018. https://genius.com/Phillips-craig-and-dean-favorite-song-of-all-lyrics.